Caribbean

by
EMMA STANFORD

PASSPORT BOOKS
a division of *NTC Publishing Group*
Lincolnwood, Illinois USA

Published by Passport Books, a division of NTC Publishing Group, 4255 West Touhy Avenue, Lincolnwood (Chicago), Illinois 60646–1975 U.S.A.

Copyright © 1997 by the Automobile Association

ALL RIGHTS RESERVED. NO PART OF THIS BOOK MAY BE REPRODUCED IN ANY FORM OR BY ANY ELECTRONIC OR MECHANICAL MEANS, INCLUDING INFORMATION STORAGE AND RETRIEVAL SYSTEMS, WITHOUT PERMISSION IN WRITING FROM THE PUBLISHERS, EXCEPT BY A REVIEWER WHO MAY QUOTE BRIEF PASSAGES IN A REVIEW.

The contents of this publication are believed correct at the time of printing. Nevertheless, the publishers cannot accept responsibility for errors or omissions, nor for changes in details given. We are always grateful to readers who let us know of any errors or omissions they come across, and future printings will be updated accordingly.

Published by Passport Books in conjunction with The Automobile Association of Great Britain.

Written by Emma Stanford
"Peace and Quiet" section by Paul Sterry

Library of Congress Catalog
Card Number 96–70461
ISBN 0–8442–4814–2

10 9 8 7 6 5 4 3 2 1

PRINTED IN TRENTO, ITALY

Front cover picture: Barbados – boat and beach

Contents

This book employs a simple rating system to help choose which places to visit:

	'top ten'

◆◆◆   do not miss
◆◆   see if you can
◆   worth seeing if you have time

Introduction and Background

INTRODUCTION

Coconut palms and sandy beaches, azure seas and Planter's Punch, the Caribbean leaps out of the travel poster and into three-dimensional reality at the foot of the gangplank. Since Christopher Columbus first brought news of their existence to the Spanish court, these delectable, sun-kissed islands have worked their magic on generations of travellers and tourists.

For most visitors a Caribbean holiday is an idyllic escape from the daily grind. There is no shortage of sun, sea and sand, but look beyond the beach resort or the comfortable familiarity of the cruise ship, and the Caribbean's charms are many and varied. Each island has its own unique flavour, a combination of geography, history, culture and attitude which can come as a surprise to anyone who ever thought the Caribbean was just, well... the Caribbean.

The old colonial powers left their mark in a dozen different ways from architecture to politics and language. Former British islands, such as Antigua and Barbados, retain a wealth of solid Georgian architecture, government based on the British parliamentary model, red telephone boxes and cricket pitches; the Spanish Catholic heritage is alive and well in Puerto Rico; the Dutch transformed Curaçao's waterfront into a tropical Amsterdam of pastel-painted gabled façades; and in Guadeloupe and Martinique, French language, culinary traditions and *savoir-faire* are very much the

Palm-fringed Dark Wood Beach, Antigua – proof that the Caribbean really does live up to its idyllic image

INTRODUCTION

English Harbour, Antigua, is one of the best natural harbours in the Caribbean

order of the day. More recently, America has stepped in to transform the US Virgin Islands (where the Danes once built marzipan-coloured fortresses) into one of the richest and most developed corners of the region.

Local scenery is equally diverse and often stunningly beautiful. Towering volcanic peaks cloaked in luxuriant rainforest are juxtaposed with blinding white sand strands barely rising above sea level. There are waterfalls and mountains, sulphurous hot springs and desert landscapes, spice plantations and brilliant tropical plants sprouting exuberantly by the roadside. Even below the surface of the waves the marine landscape continues to dazzle with its vivid array of corals and tropical fish.

Perfect Caribbean holidays come in all shapes and sizes, but an essential ingredient for success is choosing the right island (or combination of islands). To help you make that choice, and make the best of your stay, this guide covers some 40 of the best Caribbean islands, from action-packed Jamaica to laid-back Nevis, and from glamorous jet-set St Barts to low-key, eco-friendly Grenada, plus ever-popular (though non-Caribbean) cruise-ship favourites, the Bahamas and Bermuda.

BACKGROUND

Geography

The Caribbean archipelago stretches in an arc almost 2,500 miles (4,000km) long from Cuba, which lies 90 miles (145km) south of Key West on the southern tip of Florida, to Trinidad, just off the coast of Venezuela. South of the Tropic of Cancer (which passes through the Bahamas), the necklace of 7,000-plus islands, cays (islets), coral atolls and reefs is buffeted on the north and east by the Atlantic Ocean, and encircles the million-square-mile (2.6 million sq km) Caribbean Sea.

The Antilles

Early explorers christened the entire archipelago the Antilles, but the islands are now grouped into the Greater Antilles (Puerto Rico to Cuba in the north), and the Lesser Antilles. From Trinidad, the Lesser Antilles curve up and around through the Windward and Leeward Islands, interspersed by the French Antilles and the smaller islands of the Netherlands Antilles, to the Virgin Islands. Barbados stands off on its own to the east of the Windwards, while the Dutch ABCs (Aruba, Bonaire and Curaçao), the main islands of the Netherlands Antilles, lie west of Trinidad along the Venezuelan coast.

For the purposes of this guide, the Bahama Islands, scattered across 100,000 square miles (260,000sq km) of the Atlantic southeast of Florida, are included in our round-up, as is far-flung Bermuda, 1,000 miles (1,600km) to the north.

Volcanic origins

The region is poised on the brink of the Caribbean and Atlantic tectonic plates, and the majority of the islands are of volcanic origin with a few low-lying coral atolls such as the Cayman Islands and Anguilla. There are imposing mountain ranges in Jamaica and Puerto Rico, while Guadeloupe, Martinique, St Vincent, Montserrat, Dominica and St Lucia are all still volcanically active and ooze with boiling mud pools and smelly sulphur springs.

Giant palmferns in St Lucia's rainforest

BACKGROUND

Statue of Columbus at St Ann's Bay, Jamaica, where the explorer and his crew were shipwrecked in 1502

History

More than 2,000 years before Columbus first sighted the Bahamas, on 12 October 1492, Amerindian tribes began migrating to the Caribbean islands from South America. The peaceable Arawak tribes Columbus initially encountered had inhabited the region for a thousand years, but had recently come under threat from warlike Carib Indians, after whom the region is named.

Spanish gold

Columbus' mission to find a western route to the East Indian spice islands was a failure, but he doggedly named his Caribbean finds the West Indies. More importantly, the explorer located the South American mainland on his fourth voyage in 1502, and secured its vast riches for the Catholic kings of Spain. Within a few years, the Spanish colonies on Hispaniola, Puerto Rico, Cuba and Jamaica had decimated the Arawak population through disease, warfare and transportation to work the mainland gold mines. Settlers later drove the Caribs from the Windward 'Cannibal Isles'. For pirates and privateers, the heavily-laden Spanish treasure ships were tempting targets, and they harried them mercilessly throughout the 16th and 17th centuries operating out of the isolated cays of the Bahamas, the Virgin Islands and the notorious pirate capital of Port Royal in Jamaica.

Sugar and slavery

The Spanish imported the first African slaves to the New World as early as 1517, but it was the explosion of the sugar trade in the mid-1600s which led to the large-scale colonisation of the Caribbean islands and inspired the infamous 'triangular trade'. To operate labour-intensive but hugely profitable sugar cane plantations, a massive workforce was required, and preferably one suited to the tropics. The answer lay in West Africa, where European manufactured goods could be exchanged for slaves who were then shipped on the notorious 'Middle Passage' to the West Indies; the holds were then loaded with sugar for the voyage back to Europe.

The Caribbean slave trade was the largest forced transportation of human beings in history. It is estimated that some 40 million Africans were transported in 250 years. One in eight died on the Middle Passage, and those that survived the eight-week voyage were sold at auction and subjugated to a back-breaking regime of work, beatings and regulations designed to break their spirit and links to African culture.

During the heyday of the plantation era, the Caribbean region was anything but stable. Far-off conflicts in Europe were mirrored in the colonies, where Spanish influence declined, while British and French colonists squabbled incessantly, and gained, lost and regained island territories with bewildering frequency. By the start of the 19th century, the writing was on the wall for Caribbean sugar as the introduction of sugar beet in Europe drained the colonists' profits. The abolition movement, championed by Granville Sharp, Thomas Clarkson and William Wilberforce in Britain, and by Victor Schoelcher in France, added to the pressure, and Britain finally abolished slavery in 1838, followed by France in 1848.

From emancipation to independence

With the loss of the sugar trade, the islands fell into decline. Newly-emancipated slaves abandoned the remaining plantations, and islands such as Jamaica and Trinidad turned to the East Indies as a source of indentured labour. The Spanish–American War in 1898 introduced US influence to the region in Puerto Rico. In 1917, America purchased the US Virgin Islands from Denmark.

The effects of the 1930s depression trickled through to the Caribbean causing severe economic problems and triggering the rise of the labour movements which would lead the transition towards independence among former British colonies during the 1950s and '60s. Several of the smaller islands opted to remain British Crown Colonies, while others have joined the British Commonwealth as independent island states. The Dutch and French continue to maintain territories in the Lesser Antilles.

*Mounted policeman
in Jamaica*

Problems in paradise

Though for the most part remarkably stable, the deeply fragmented Caribbean political scene has proved a severe drawback when trying to redress social and economic problems in the region. Suspicion and self-interest have largely thwarted the Caribbean Community (Caricom) in its attempts to hammer out a common policy. Tourism is vital to the local economy, but the ever-widening gap between the haves and the have-nots causes considerable friction, and many resent the low-spending cruise ship visitors and holiday-makers sequestered in all-inclusive resorts, seeing them as a threat rather than a boon to local businesses.

Culture

The Caribbean heritage is an exotic hybrid derived from over five centuries of cross-cultural pollination. The mosques and curries of Trinidad's East Indian community sit alongside tropical Anglican churches, where West African rhythms hijack Baptist hymns, and the world-famous Carnival is known as *mas* from the *masquerades*, or pre-Lenten parties and masked balls, first thrown by French Catholic settlers in the 18th century. Every aspect of local life from music and language (see page 124) to religion and cooking (see pages 103–4) is a complex fusion of many different influences.

Religion

Religion still plays an important part in island life. As a rule of thumb, the former British colonies are Protestant, with a high preponderance of Baptist, Methodist and evangelical churches, while the Spanish and French islands are Roman Catholic. However, several African animist traditions have survived the centuries of Christian teaching, and visitors at carnival time will see stilt-wearing *jumby* or *duppy* (restless ghost) figures joining in the processions. Rastafarianism, which originated in Jamaica during the 1930s as disillusioned young West Indians turned away from Western culture to Africa in the search for identity, is also widespread throughout the region.

Bob Marley, international reggae star and Jamaican national hero

Music

Music is the heartbeat of the Caribbean and its most famous export in modern times. You can't go far in the Caribbean without being assailed by the infectious rhythms of reggae. Its greatest exponent, Jamaica's Bob Marley (1945–81), is a local legend. Meanwhile, the origins of calypso can be traced back to the plantation era and the West African story-telling tradition. A potent combination of oral history, political and social comment plus a healthy dose of gossip and humour, calypso is a force to be reckoned with and its biggest stars, such as Mighty Sparrow, are revered.

What to See

The Essential rating system:

✓	'top ten'

◆◆◆   do not miss
◆◆   see if you can
◆   worth seeing if you
         have time

This guide does not attempt to cover every Caribbean island nor every sightseeing opportunity. Instead it concentrates on a selection of the top holiday destinations, cruise-ship ports and attractions throughout the region, with additional information covering the Bahama Islands to the north, as well as Bermuda.

As a rule, the islands of the Lesser Antilles have been listed alphabetically under their main south-to-north island groupings: the Windward Islands (Dominica, Grenada, St Lucia, St Vincent and the Grenadines); the Leeward Islands (Anguilla, Antigua, Montserrat, St Kitts and Nevis); and the British and US Virgin Islands. The politically united but geographically scattered French Antilles (Guadeloupe, Martinique, St Barts), and the Netherlands Antilles (Aruba, Bonaire, Curaçao, Saba, Sint Eustatius and Sint Maarten/Saint-Martin, the latter a joint Dutch–French territory) are also grouped together, as are the main Bahama Islands. The final

category features other cruising islands (Barbados, Bermuda, the Cayman Islands, Jamaica, Puerto Rico, Trinidad and Tobago). Each island has its own entry with a short introduction and a description of the main town, followed by an A–Z gazetteer covering the island's chief attractions. These are by necessity brief, but designed to give visitors an overview of what to see.

Do remember when planning around-island excursions to leave plenty of time. Although distances are short, Caribbean travel times are often at least double what you might expect. Road warnings are often pretty cavalier (or non-existant) too, so it is easy to get lost. The best advice is to hire a local taxi driver (see page 121), agree a price for a tour and the duration.

Information on opening times etc has been provided for guidance only. We have tried to ensure accuracy, but things do change and we would advise readers to check locally before planning visits to avoid any possible disappointment.

The volcanic plug of Petit Piton on St Lucia

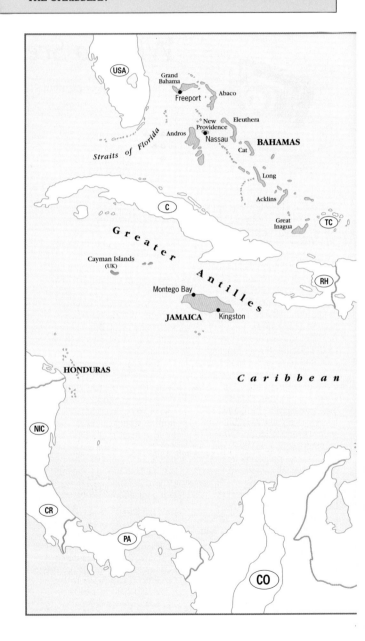

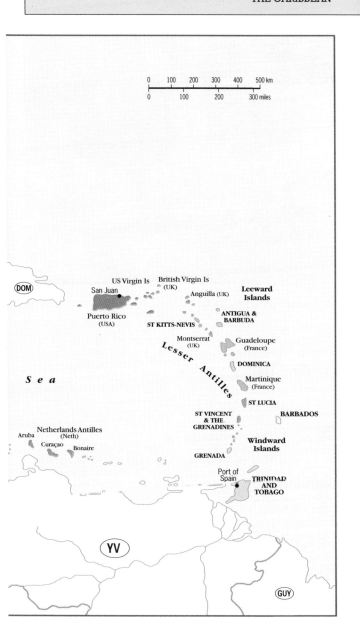

0   100   200   300   400   500 km
0   100   200   300 miles

US Virgin Is   British Virgin Is
(UK)
San Juan   Anguilla (UK)   **Leeward
Islands**

Puerto Rico
(USA)   **ANTIGUA &
BARBUDA**
(DOM)

ST KITTS-NEVIS

Montserrat   Guadeloupe
(UK)   (France)

Lesser Antilles

DOMINICA

S e a   Martinique
(France)

ST LUCIA

**ST VINCENT
& THE   BARBADOS
GRENADINES**

Netherlands Antilles
(Neth)   **Windward
Aruba   Islands**
Curaçao   Bonaire

GRENADA

Port of
Spain   **TRINIDAD
AND
TOBAGO**

(YV)

(GUY)

THE WINDWARD ISLANDS

THE WINDWARD ISLANDS

A Roseau market trader displays her wares

DOMINICA

Rising steeply from the ocean to the peak of Morne Diablotin at 4,747 feet (1,447m), mountainous and rainforested Dominica (pronounced *Domin-eeker*) is known as the 'Nature Island of the Caribbean'. For several hundred years after its discovery by Columbus in 1493, Dominica was branded one of the 'Cannibal Isles' inhabited by Carib Indians, and given a wide berth by early colonists. The region's last Caribs survive here, and it was once a haven for escaped slaves.

Dominica is ruggedly beautiful with an all-but-impenetrable jungle interior scoured by deep valleys and irrigated by dozens of rivers and waterfalls. Topography has kept development at bay, and the island has few beaches (but great diving). Agriculture is still the mainstay of the island's economy, but recently Dominica has introduced low-key tourism and most visitors come here to enjoy one of the last unspoilt corners of the Caribbean.

ROSEAU

The island's pint-sized capital sits at the mouth of the Roseau river, guarded by the remains of 18th-century Fort Young. The bustling streets are lined by weatherbeaten wooden buildings, many festooned with gingerbread decoration, and there is a lively local produce market down by the river.

At the southern end of town, the Gothic-style Cathedral of the Assumption stands on a small hill. It is an easy stroll east from here to the 40-acre (16ha) Botanical Gardens, where more than 150 species of plants and trees flourish on the site of an old sugar plantation.

> **Rare Birds**
> Dominica boasts two native parrot species found nowhere else in the world. Both the 20-inch- (50cm) high Sisserou parrot (*Amazona imperialis*), the largest Amazon parrot, and the Jaco (or red-necked parrot, *Amazona arausiaca*) are endangered, but they may be spotted in the Northern Forest Reserve, or in the aviary at Roseau's Botanical Gardens.

◆◆
CABRITS NATIONAL PARK
2 miles (3.2km) north of Portsmouth
Jutting out from the northwest coast, the park occupies a peninsula sheltering Prince Rupert Bay, where Sir Francis Drake would stop off to resupply his ships. The ruins of Fort Shirley (dating from 1765) are dotted around the hillside site. Offshore, an underwater trail provides excellent snorkelling in a 790-acre (320ha) marine reserve.

◆
INDIAN RIVER and PORTSMOUTH
Portsmouth is the island's second town (and former capital), but not a place to spend much time. However, just south of town, there are boat trips up the Indian river, where Carib Indians used to paddle upstream through the shady,

green tunnel of overhanging vegetation to reach their settlements tucked back from the coast.

◆◆◆
MORNE TROIS PITONS NATIONAL PARK
from Laudat, 7 miles (11km) east of Roseau
A sprawling 17,000-acre (7,000ha) tract of Dominica's mountainous highlands, the park's primordial rainforest is sprinkled with mountain lakes, sulphur springs and, almost invariably, rain. Despite the frequent showers, this is magnificent hiking country with easy trails leading to the Freshwater Lake and Boeri Lake, and more challenging hikes to the volcanic Boiling Lake and to the Valley of Desolation, where active fumaroles hiss with sulphurous gas. Many island tours include the short off-road walk to the crystal-clear Emerald Pool, in a pretty grotto fed by a miniature waterfall.

◆◆
NORTHERN FOREST RESERVE
On the lush, jungle-cloaked slopes of Morne Diablotin, the 22,000-acre (8,900ha) forest reserve was established in 1952, and is a refuge for the island's rare parrots (see box). Diablotin is the second highest peak in the Lesser Antilles and a challenging hike, but there is a short nature trail from the Syndicate Estate, an old citrus and banana plantation 1,800 feet (550m) up the northwest flank, which winds through the rainforest with plenty of opportunities for plant and birdlife spotting.

THE WINDWARD ISLANDS

TRAFALGAR FALLS
Roseau Valley, east of Roseau
Actually part of the Morne Trois Pitons Park, but easily accessible by bus from Roseau, the 200-foot (60m) falls plummet down the sheer cliff face in clouds of cool spray to the river below. It is a stiff hike to the lower falls, and sensible shoes are a must, particularly when following guides up to the second, higher vantage point. Then cool off by the river where the iron-rich water has streaked huge boulders in orange and black stripes.

Eating Out
Roseau's **La Robe Creole**, Fort Street (tel: 809/448 2896) is renowned for serving good island food in an attractive old colonial setting with waitresses tricked out in traditional costume. Downtown, **The Orchard**, corner of King George V and Great George Streets (tel: 809/448 3051) specialises in West Indian fare as well as hamburgers and sandwiches, as does **Callaloo**, 66 King George V Street (tel: 809/448 3386), and both offer courtyard dining. On the road to Trafalgar Falls, **Papillotte Wilderness Retreat** (tel: 809/448 2287) is deep in the tropical rainforest and also offers rooms. Dominica's smartest dining room is in the elegant **Reigate Hall Hotel**, on the hillside above Roseau (tel: 809/448 4031); while the **Layou Valley Inn**, some distance north near the Forest Reserve (tel: 809/499 6203), wins points for charm and tranquillity.

GRENADA
The Spice Island of the Caribbean, Grenada even features a nutmeg on its national flag. Measuring just 21 miles by 12 miles (34km by 19km), the island also produces cloves, cinnamon, allspice and mace, and possesses an alluring combination of rugged, rainforested hinterland and a coastline dotted with secluded coves and stretches of dazzling, sandy beach.
Grenada lies at the southern end of the Windward Islands, and was named by Spanish sailors homesick for the mountains of southern Spain (though it is pronounced *Grenayda*). The French, then the British held the island until independence in 1974. In 1983, a US 'friendly invasion' stabilised the country after left-wing leader Maurice Bishop was imprisoned and executed by members of his own People's Revolutionary Government, since when all has been quiet.

ST GEORGE'S
One of the prettiest harbours in the Caribbean, St George's nestles on the steep-sided slopes of an extinct volcanic crater. Behind the curving waterfront Carenage, where cruise ship passengers come ashore, old Georgian buildings and pastel-coloured homes clamber in a cat's-cradle of narrow streets to a ring of ruined colonial fortresses with fine views from Fort George and Fort Frederick. Across the hill on the bay side, the

National Museum features archaeological and historic artefacts laid out in an 18th-century army barracks off Young Street. But for a real slice of Grenadian life, try to catch the colourful spice and produce stalls on Market Square each Saturday.
Museum open: Monday to Friday 09.00–16.30hrs; Saturday 10.00–13.00hrs.

◆◆
CONCORD FALLS
7 miles (11km) northwest of St George's
Tumbling down the Concord Valley in the lee of Mount Qua Qua, the lowest of these three falls is a favourite stop on island tours. You can escape the crowds by hiking up to the higher falls and cooling off in the invigorating freshwater pools.

◆◆◆
DOUGALDSTON ESTATE
south of Gouyave
Pallets of cinnamon bark, mace, cocoa pods and arabica coffee drying in the sun greet visitors to the island's chief spice plantation. Take a tour of the aromatic old wooden barn and learn how the spices are still processed in time-honoured (and technology-free) fashion.
Open: Monday to Friday 09.00–16.00hrs; Saturday 10.00–13.00hrs.

◆
GOUYAVE
A dusty, small seaside town, Gouyave's main claim to fame is the Grenada Nutmeg Cooperative. This is the place

St George's waterfront Carenage hemmed in by hills

to watch nutmegs being prepared for market and learn all you ever wanted to know about mace, its waxy, red by-product and a spice in its own right.
Cooperative open: Monday to Saturday 09.00–16.00hrs.

◆◆◆
GRAND ANSE BEACH
3 miles (5km) south of St George's
This 2-mile (3km) strip of fine white sand is the island's most popular beach with several

hotels and restaurants, plus watersports facilities. There is a convenient water-taxi service from the Carenage.

GRAND ETANG FOREST RESERVE
7 miles (11km) northeast of St George's
From St George's, it is a steep 15-minute drive up to the Forest Reserve. Here, the Annandale Falls cascade 30 feet (9m) down into a swimming hole edged by giant ferns and creepers. A few miles on, several trails lead off into the rainforest from a roadside information centre. It is only a short walk to Grand Etang, a 30-acre (12ha) crater lake some 1,740 feet (530m) above sea level.

LA SAGESSE NATURE CENTRE
9 miles (14km) east of St George's
Three beautiful beaches, reef diving, and birdwatching in a rich estuarine mangrove belt are all part of La Sagesse's appeal. This former private estate in the isolated southeast corner of the island also offers trails through woodland and scrub cactus areas, and a short hike along the river bank to the Marquis River waterfall.

SAUTEURS/CARIB'S LEAP
20 miles (32km) north of St George's
Behind the village of Sauteurs (translating as 'leapers' or 'jumpers' from the French), a section of the sheer north coast cliffs is known as Carib's Leap.

In 1651, the last of Grenada's Carib Indians preferred to take this suicidal 100-foot (30m) leap down to the ocean rather than submit to French rule.
East of Sauteurs, Levera National Park offers walking trails and a superb beach, plus snorkelling in the pristine waters of Levera Bay.

Carriacou
A short hop to the north of Grenada, Carriacou is the largest of the Grenadines, and an occasional cruise ship stop. Hillsborough is the main town with a small Historical Society Museum, Paterson Street, laid out in a restored 19th-century cotton mill. The islanders are excellent boat-builders, and their graceful wooden schooners can be seen tied up along the waterfront.

Eating Out
Right on the Carenage in St George's, **The Nutmeg** (tel: 809/440 2539) is a good spot to watch the world overlooking the waterfront. **Mamma's Restaurant & Bar**, Lagoon Road (tel: 809/440 1459) is another popular local eatery. For upmarket dining at Grand Anse, check out the terrace dining room at **La Belle Creole**, Blue Horizons Hotel (tel: 809/444 4316), and **Canboulay** (tel: 809/444 4401). An absolute must when touring the island is Betty Mascoll's **Morne Fondue**, south of Sauteurs (tel: 809/442 9330), for West Indian pepperpot stew served up in a modest and splendidly old-fashioned plantation house set in the hills with gardens and a couple of simple rooms.

ST LUCIA

St Lucia (pronounced *Loo-sha*) is a real Caribbean beauty from the tips of her twin volcanic peaks, the Pitons, to the soft, sandy beaches fringing the northwest coast. As well as providing a visual treat, St Lucia is also one of the friendliest islands around, with a famous all-comers-welcome 'jump-up' street party held every Friday night in the village of Gros Islet. The British and French tussled over St Lucia for a century and a half before Britain got the upper hand in 1814. However, the islanders still speak a French-based *patois*, and the food is above average here, too. Agriculture remains an important element of the island economy, with acres of banana plantations unfurling along the east coast, but tourism is gradually taking over. Fortunately, development is largely confined to the northwest.

◆
CASTRIES

The island's uninspiring capital was rebuilt after a major fire in 1948. However, the **Central Market**, on Jeremie Street, is a good place to snap up local colour. Near by, the interior of the 1897 **Cathedral of the Immaculate Conception** in Derek Walcott Square (named for St Lucia's Nobel Prize-winning poet), is decorated with biblical murals.

Behind the town centre, several old Caribbean houses have been preserved on the slopes of Morne Fortune, along with the remains of 18th-century Fort Charlotte, and the Inniskilling Memorial, which commemorates the British troops who captured the hill from the French in 1796.

◆
CENTRAL RAINFOREST RESERVE

central Highlands, access from Fond St-Jaques (southeast of Soufrière)

The Forestry Division maintains a number of trails through the central uplands with terrific views across to the Pitons and Mount Gimie (3,116ft/950m), the island's highest peak. This is one of the last refuges of the endangered St Lucia parrot, and permission is required to hike here.

Open: daily, with permission from the Foresty Department (tel: 758/450 2231).

Sun umbrellas and colourful produce stalls in Castries Market

Lovely Marigot Bay's sheltered yacht anchorage

◆◆
DIAMOND MINERAL BATHS AND BOTANICAL GARDENS

2 miles (3km) southeast of Soufrière
Fed by an underground spring from the Soufrière volcano, the mineral baths were built for French king Louis XVI's troops in 1785. The warm, milky-grey waters are not very enticing, but the surrounding tropical gardens are spectacular.
Open: daily, 10.00–17.00hrs.

◆◆
MARIGOT BAY

8 miles (13km) south of Castries
Marigot Bay's picture-perfect harbour inlet is a favourite movie location with a yacht marina, attractive resort, and a strip of sandy beach fringed by palm trees and reached by a tiny ferry from the boat dock.

views out to sea and off to the Pitons. An interpretation centre has been laid out in the 18th-century former Officers' Mess; there is a botanical trail around the grassy slopes; and a waterfront café overlooking the beach.
Open: daily, 09.00–17.00hrs. Guided tours available.

◆◆◆
THE PITONS
southwest coast
The best views of the jagged Pitons ('peaks' in French) are from the sea – which is an advantage for cruise ship passengers. Thought to have been created by volcanic activity around 15,000 years ago, **Gros Piton** (2,618ft/798m) and **Petit Piton** (2,461ft/750m) rise dramatically sheer from the shore and also make impressive viewing from the coast road above Soufrière.

◆◆
RODNEY BAY
8 miles (13km) north of Castries
A haven for yachtsmen, Rodney Bay offers a good selection of pubs and restaurants, and several of the island's best hotels line the beach here.

◆◆◆
PIGEON ISLAND NATIONAL HISTORIC PARK
northwest coast
Humpbacked Pigeon Island was supposedly named after the pigeon message service operated by lookouts stationed on hilltop Fort Rodney. The British naval hero, Admiral Rodney, kept an eye on the French fleet from the ruined fort, which still affords fantastic

◆◆
SOUFRIÈRE TOWN and LA SOUFRIÈRE VOLCANO
southwest coast
A weatherbeaten seaside village, Soufrière is the jumping off point for St Lucia's 'drive-in volcano'. Cars can drive up to within a few hundred yards (metres) of La Soufrière's steaming sulphur hot springs. The mineral-rich volcanic brew bubbles and

oozes in a sinister fashion creating multicoloured deposits of copper, iron, magnesium and reeking yellow sulphur. Local guides regale visitors with facts and gory stories.
La Soufriére open: daily, 09.00–17.00hrs.

THE SOUTH COAST

Several unassuming small fishing villages dot the coast beyond Soufrière. **Choiseul** is a great place to pick up local crafts at bargain prices from the Arts & Crafts Development Centre. **Vieux Fort** is the departure point for the **Maria Islands Nature Reserve**, a seabird and turtle nesting site. You can also watch frigate birds nesting on the east coast's **Frigate Island** from an observation point off the main road.

Eating Out

A local institution on the hillside above Castries, the **Green Parrot**, Morne Fortune (tel: 758/452 3399) serves up international and West Indian cuisine with views. **Jimmie's**, Vigie Harbour (tel: 758/452 5142) has a great harbourfront position, and **The Charthouse**, Rodney Bay (tel: 758/452 8115) is a yachtie favourite overlooking the water; both do a good line in seafood. Near by, **The Lime**, Rodney Bay (tel: 758/452 0761) is a relaxed and friendly spot serving burgers, salads and local dishes. For something rather special, **San Antoine**, Morne Fortune (tel: 758/452 4660) offers fine dining in a lovely old colonial house with tremendous views.

ST VINCENT AND THE GRENADINES

Heading the 60-mile (95km) chain of Grenadine Islands, which trail south to Grenada, St Vincent is a luxuriantly tropical backwater. Its thickly forested, mountainous interior once provided sanctuary to indigenous 'Yellow Caribs', runaway slaves, and their descendants, the 'Black Caribs', whose ferocious defence of their territory kept colonists at bay right up to the mid-18th century. When the Caribs were finally defeated, the British took control and planted sugar cane, arrowroot and Sea Island cotton in the accessible valleys.

St Vincent's rich, volcanic soil is so fertile they say you could plant a pencil here and it would grow. Agriculture remains the mainstay of the local economy, particularly bananas, coconuts and other fruits such as guava, papaya and avocado pears grown in the Mesopotamia Valley. A handful of small hotels spread along the south coast close to the capital, Kingstown, but most of St Vincent's airport arrivals push straight on to the beaches and yachting centres of the Grenadines.

KINGSTOWN

A laid-back bayfront town hemmed in by mountains, Kingstown's bustling wharves are the liveliest section of the town, and the covered market generally bursts its bounds and spills out onto Market Square. There are old arcaded shopfronts dating from colonial days, and a plethora of churches. Among the most noticeable are **St George's Anglican Cathedral**, which boasts a stained-glass window featuring a red-garbed angel, supposedly commissioned by Queen Victoria who rejected it on the grounds that angels in the Bible always wear white. **St Mary's Roman Catholic Cathedral** is a positive riot of conflicting architectural styles designed by a Belgian priest who drew his inspiration from pictures of famous European cathedrals.

◆◆◆
BOTANIC GARDENS
off the Leeward Highway
East of Kingstown town centre, the oldest botanical gardens in the western hemisphere are flourishing. They were established in 1765, and once acted as a distant tropical department of Kew Gardens in London. For a couple of EC (Eastern Caribbean) dollars, guides will show visitors around some of the more bizarre and interesting species from the sealing wax palm to the exploding blooms of the cannonball tree. Particular pride is taken in the breadfruit trees introduced from Tahiti in 1793 by the infamous Captain Bligh, survivor of the mutiny on the *Bounty*.
Around the 20-acre (8ha) grounds, the former Curator's House has been transformed into a small local history museum; the Governor-General's House, at the northern end of the gardens, dates from 1835; and for a guaranteed viewing of the rare St Vincent

Tropical plants and trees in the Botanic Gardens, Kingstown

parrot follow the ear-piercing squawks to the aviary complex. *Open*: daily, dawn to dusk.

◆◆
FALLS OF BALEINE
northwest coast
Day cruises around the west coast to the falls make a popular excursion from Kingstown. The 60-foot (18m) cascade tumbles down the slopes of La Soufrière, St Vincent's slumbering volcano, and boats anchor off a black sand beach a short walk away. A 3½-mile (5.5km) walking trail leads to Soufrière's summit (4,049ft/1,234m) from the east coast of the island.

THE WINDWARD ISLANDS

FORT CHARLOTTE
1 mile (1.6km) west of central Kingstown

Perched on a hilltop high above the harbour, these crumbling battlements command magnificent views down across the Grenadines – even as far as Grenada on a clear day. The fort's rusty cannon are trained inland to the steep, folded hills indicating the defenders were more concerned with the Caribs than potential sea-borne marauders.

◆◆◆
THE GRENADINES ✓

This jewel-like chain of 30 or so tiny islands and cays (only eight of which are inhabited) is one of the most alluring yachting and island-hopping destinations in the world. Nine miles (14km) south of St Vincent, **Bequia** (pronounced *Beck-wee*) enjoys a reputation for boat-building, and sheltered Admiralty Bay is always packed with visiting yachts. The pretty town of Port Elizabeth lies on the bay with a selection of craft shops and waterfront restaurants. Water-taxis can be hired to reach the sandy shore at Princess Margaret Beach and Lower Bay. An hour's sail from Bequia, the exclusive Caribbean hideaway of **Mustique** can count Mick Jagger and Princess Margaret among its fans. The island is a private company with around 300 inhabitants who service 75 palatial holiday homes and the Cotton House hotel. There are several fine beaches and excellent snorkelling.

Quiet **Canouan** is ringed by superb beaches and the reef diving is exceptional. Yachtsmen tend to make a beeline for Grand Bay, a favourite anchorage on the leeward shore.

Mayreau is a minute scrubby dot with good beaches on the leeward coast. A stiff hike uphill from the makeshift dock to a couple of restaurants-cum-bars is rewarded with rum punch and views. Boats from Mayreau sail to the uninhabited **Tobago Cays** for the exceptional coral reef diving. **Union Island** is a transport hub for connections to the other islands, including the privately owned resorts of **Palm Island** and **Petit St Vincent** (better known as 'PSV').

Eating Out

Non-residents need permission to come ashore if they sail across to dine at St Vincent's exclusive **Young Island Resort**, Kingstown Harbour (tel: 809/458 4826), but things are rather more relaxed at **Basil's Bar**, downstairs from the Cobblestone Inn, Bay Street (tel: 809/457 2713). In the hotel district of Villa, the **French Restaurant** (tel: 809/458 4972) serves fine French and local cuisine. On Bequia, the charming **Frangipani Hotel**, Elizabeth Bay (tel: 809/458 3255) offers terrace dining on the waterfront, and **Dawn's Creole Garden**, Lower Bay (tel: 809/458 3154) serves delicious local cooking all day; **Basil's Bar** (tel: 809/458 4621) is the official jet set hang out on Mustique; and the Planter's Punch at **Dennis' Hideaway** on Mayreau makes the hill-climb worthwhile.

THE LEEWARD ISLANDS

ANGUILLA

A low-lying, coral limestone strand at the northern tip of the Leeward Islands, Anguilla (the 'eel') measures 16 miles by 3 miles (25km by 5km), and can boast some 30 stunning beaches and sandy coves that are reckoned to be the finest in the Caribbean. The shallow, turquoise sea is a snorkeller's delight, and natural offshore reef areas have been augmented with scuttled vessels to provide additional dive sites.

Anguilla was once a pirate haven and, having few natural

Rendezvous Bay: life is a beach on Anguilla

resources, the early settlers were adventurous traders, shipbuilders and carpenters. Lumped together with St Kitts and Nevis by the British administration, the Anguillans rebelled when their neighbours looked like achieving independence, and staged a mini-revolution in 1967, which secured the island British Crown Colony status.

Boat-building is still a local money-earner, as is fishing, but tourism is the real name of the game on Anguilla. The island is renowned for its exclusive and expensive resort hotels, though the atmosphere is distinctly low key. There are daily ferries (20 minutes) to the fleshpots of Sint Maarten/Saint-Martin for shopping, otherwise life is pretty much a beach on Anguilla.

THE VALLEY
Anguilla's diminutive capital offers all the usual administrative buildings, the hospital, and a few art galleries and shops.

CAPTAIN'S BAY
northeast coast
One of several secluded bays on the northeast coast of the island. **Savannah Bay**, to the south, is another quiet, development-free spot.

LITTLE BAY
central north coast
The best way to get to this isolated sandy cove is by boat, but hardy types can trek in down the cliffs which are dotted with caves.

RENDEZVOUS BAY
southwest coast
A 2-mile (3km) swathe of powder-soft sand edging the gently curved bayfront, Rendezvous is a good place to walk and watch pelicans skimming the waves in search of dinner. Neighbouring **Cove Bay** is a smaller, less visited version.

SHOAL BAY
north coast
One of Anguilla's most spectacular beaches, and therefore definitely in the Caribbean's Top Five. Snorkel gear is available for hire, along with all the accoutrements of a deluxe day by the beach (umbrellas, sunloungers, beach towels – the lot). A couple of hotels and bars provide respite from the rays.

Eating Out
Sandy Ground, Anguilla's main port on the central north coast, is the island's 'Restaurant Row'. Try **Lucy's Harbour View** (tel: 809/497 6253) for generous West Indian cuisine; or **Riviera** (tel: 809/497 2833). In the south, **Mango's**, Barnes Bay (tel: 809/497 6497) serves delicious **New American** fare. South coast favourite, **Smuggler's Restaurant**, Forest Bay (tel: 809/497 3728), demonstrates a French influence and does great things with seafood (Anguilla's fresh-caught spiny lobsters are flown to restaurants around the Caribbean).
NB It is only necessary to dial the last four digits of telephone numbers on the island.

ANTIGUA

Like Anguilla, and its sister island of Barbuda to the north, Antigua (pronounced *An-teega*) is an arid limestone coral island ringed by gorgeous white sand beaches. The locals claim there are 365 of them – a beach for every day of the year. As the largest of the Leeward Islands (108 square miles/280sq km), Antigua is more visited and developed than its neighbours, and is a major yachting centre. The high point of the sailing calendar is April's Race Week. Columbus sighted Antigua in 1493, and named it Santa María de la Antigua after a miraculous statue of the Virgin in Seville Cathedral. With the exception of brief incursions by the Spanish and French, the British held the island from 1632 until independence in 1981. During the 18th and 19th centuries, the British navy made full use of Antigua's strategically-important, safe anchorages at Falmouth and English Harbour, and settlers planted the island with sugar cane from end to end. Antigua's dry, scrubby interior is still dotted with the ruins of old sugar mills.

ST JOHN'S

The island's port capital has undergone an unprecedented facelift in recent years, notably down on the waterfront where smart new cruise ship facilities and duty-free shops have sprung up on Heritage Quay. Redcliffe Quay, one block over, is lined with attractively restored old wooden buildings with a more interesting selection of shops. The town was laid out in 1702,

Pubbing in Antigua

and backs up the hill from the waterfront towards the silver-topped towers of 19th-century St John's Cathedral. At the corner of Market and Long Streets, the **Museum of Antigua and Barbuda** occupies the Old Court House built in 1750. Stop in for an introduction to local

---

Trade Winds

Brewed up in the high pressure area of the mid-Atlantic, the cooling trade winds blow down towards the equator, fanning the Caribbean islands as they go. While they reduce the temperature, they also carry in the clouds which release precipitation on the thirsty upland rainforests. On occasions when the northern and southern trade winds meet out in the Atlantic they can spark off a hurricane, and throughout the tropical summer Caribbean islanders pay attention to the local adage: 'June, too soon; July, stand by; August, come it must; September, remember; October, all over'. In truth, most hurricanes occur in mid-September.

history and culture ranging from pre-Columbian artefacts left by the island's original Siboney and Arawak inhabitants to Viv Richards' cricket bat. The former captain of both the Antiguan and West Indian cricket teams is a national hero.
Museum open: Monday to Thursday 08.30–16.30hrs; Friday 08.30–16.00hrs; Saturday 10.00–14.00hrs.

BETTY'S HOPE
Pares Village (central island road)
The Betty's Hope plantation was established in 1674, and grew into one of Antigua's main sugar producers. The mill ruins are being slowly restored, and a visitors' centre houses a small historical museum and a shop.
Museum open: Tuesday to Saturday 09.00–17.00hrs.

DARK WOOD BEACH
near Crab Hill (southwest coast)
A dazzling crescent of pale sand lapped by azure sea and

Antigua is one of the Caribbean's top yachting destinations

fringed by palm trees, Dark Wood is irresistible. Visit on a weekday and it is virtually deserted, but things hot up considerably on the weekend.

◆◆
DEVIL'S BRIDGE
1½ miles (2.5km) east of Indian Town (northwest coast)
Hollowed out of the limestone cliffs by crashing Atlantic surf, this natural arch is a popular tourist site on round-island tours. On a blustery day the waves are forced up blowholes in the rock creating waterspouts.

◆◆
DICKENSON BAY
3 miles (5km) north of St John's
Antigua's premier tourist beach is a lively spot with resort hotels lining the sands. There is watersports equipment for hire, including windsurfers and sailing boats, also a number of beach bars and restaurants.

◆◆◆ ENGLISH HARBOUR and NELSON'S DOCKYARD

south coast
The original capital of Antigua was established at Falmouth Harbour on a broad south coast bay, which remains a popular yachting centre. Across a narrow isthmus, the sheltered, virtually landlocked confines of English Harbour represented one of the best and safest anchorages in the world, and the British navy established their chief Caribbean dockyard here in the 18th century.

Horatio Nelson spent a miserable posting in Antigua between 1784 and 1787. As captain of HMS *Boreas*, his duties included trying to stamp out the region's profitable trade with newly-independent America, incurring the wrath of local planters. He would probably be dismayed to learn that his former stamping ground, this 'vile spot' as he called it, has been named in his memory.

Restored in the 1960s, the neat stone and wood Georgian buildings of Nelson's Dockyard are now a major tourist attraction. The old naval stores have been turned into the Admiral's Inn; there is a museum in the Admiral's House; the Copper & Lumber Store is a rollicking yachtie pub and hotel; and the Officers' Quarters house shops and galleries. Across the harbour, **Clarence House**, built for the Duke of Clarence (a naval contemporary of Nelson, and later William IV of England), is the Governor-General's country retreat, open to the public when GG is not in residence.

◆◆ FIG TREE DRIVE

south of All Saints
The road from All Saints down to the coast meanders through a rare pocket of natural vegetation which escaped the sugar boom land clearances of the 17th and 18th centuries. There are lovely views down to the coast, banana plants, mango and palm trees line the road, and there is a bat cave in the forest.

◆◆ HARMONY HALL

east coast
Off the beaten track, but well worth a visit, this restored mill complex has been transformed into a gallery displaying attractive Caribbean arts and crafts and a restaurant which makes a welcome lunch stop.
Open: daily, 10.00–18.00hrs.

◆◆◆ SHIRLEY HEIGHTS

east of English Harbour
The British fortified the high ground above English Harbour, and named this sprawling hilltop military complex after General Sir Thomas Shirley, Governor of the Leeward Islands between 1781 and 1791. The site commands superb views over the island and south to Guadeloupe. There are numerous old ruins to explore and a pub-restaurant in the former Guard House at Shirley Heights Lookout, which hosts a lively Sunday brunch. A short sound-and-light show at the

Dow's Hill Interpretation Centre provides a potted history of Antigua from the original Amerindian settlers up to the present day, and there are more views from the ruins of the adjacent 18th-century governor's residence, the Belvedere.

Interpretation Centre open: daily, 09.00–17.00hrs.

Eating Out

In St John's, a short step from Heritage Quay, the veranda at **Hemingway's**, St Mary Street (tel: 268/462 2763) is a good spot for cool drinks or a light lunch with a view of the town centre; **The Lemon Tree**, Long Street (tel: 268/462 1969) is also a pleasant local joint. English Harbour has a selection of good pubs and restaurants from laid-back **Nations**, with its small garden and local cuisine, to the waterfront **Admiral's Inn**, Nelson's Dockyard (tel: 268/460 1027), or more elegant (and expensive) **La Perruche** (tel: 268/460 3040), serving French and West Indian cuisine. **G&T's** at the Antigua Yacht Club, Falmouth Harbour (tel: 268/460 3278) serves good times and pub grub to legions of yachting types; and Sunday brunch at the **Shirley Heights Lookout** (tel: 268/460 1785) is a rumbustious affair which carries on until sunset. On the north coast, **Le Bistro**, Hodges Bay (tel: 268/462 3881) is renowned for upmarket French cuisine, while Dickenson Bay's hotels provide plenty of dining opportunities, and **Miller's By the Sea** (tel: 268/462 2393) can usually be relied upon for live entertainment.

MONTSERRAT

After dry, low-lying Antigua, Montserrat's rugged volcanic highlands scoured with deep *ghauts* (river ravines) and cloaked with rainforest make a startling contrast. The island is also considerably smaller at 11 miles by 7 miles (17km by 11km), quieter and more easy-going, with only a few beaches along the leeward shore. Montserrat is the Caribbean's very own 'Emerald Isle'. During the 1630s, Irish Catholics from St Kitts and Nevis settled here to escape religious persecution. The islanders, proud of their Irish links, have adopted the shamrock as the national emblem and adorn local postage stamps with an Irish harp.

◆◆
PLYMOUTH

The sleepy, bayfront capital on the southwest coast springs to life every Saturday as local smallholders gather at the Public Market to preside over sprawling piles of fruit and vegetables, and exchange the week's gossip. Above town, the overgrown ruins of 18th-century **Fort St George** make a good lookout point.

To the south, in the Wapping district, **Government House** is the Governor's official residence set in attractive lawned gardens. The central gable of the balconied Creole mansion sports a shamrock, and visitors can inspect the interior which displays collections of island artefacts and furniture.

Government House open: for guided tours, weekdays except Wednesday, 10.30hrs–noon.

Gingerbread and bougainvillaea at Government House in Montserrat

♦
FOX'S BAY
3 miles (5km) northwest of Plymouth
Birdwatchers will find plenty to look at on a visit to this 15-acre (6ha) coastal mangrove swamp reserve. Follow beach or backwater trails and look out for herons, kingfishers, gallinules and other waterfowl.

♦♦
GALWAY'S ESTATE
3 miles (5km) south of Plymouth
In the 17th and 18th centuries, the Galway family of County Cork established a sugar dynasty based on this former 1,300-acre (525ha) estate and plantations on several other islands. Today the ruined Georgian great house, mill buildings and even an old rum still are part of a project to develop the site as an historic and cultural centre illustrating 18th-century plantation life.

♦♦
GALWAY'S SOUFRIÈRE
inland on Old Fort Road from St Patrick's (southwest coast)
Just south of Chances Peak (3,002ft/915m), Montserrat's highest point, the Soufrière is the most accessible of the island's volcanic craters. A 20-minute hike off the road leads to an area of smelly, steaming sulphur vents where boiling mud heaves and pops releasing clouds of steam and the odd rock. There is a trail up Chances Peak from the Parsons road.

THE LEEWARD ISLANDS

◆
GREAT ALPS WATERFALL
*Trail Old Fort Road, near
St Patrick's*
It is a 45-minute rainforest trek
through woodlands, past giant
ferns and colourful stands of
lobster claw heliconia
(Montserrat's national flower) to
these 70-foot (20m) cascades.
Best in the rainy season when
the waters are in full spate.

◆
MONTSERRAT MUSEUM
*Richmond Hill (northeast of
Plymouth)*
Among the local history exhibits

*In the pink: restored local
architecture in Plymouth*

on display in this restored sugar
mill are relics from pre-
Columbian settlements on
Alliouagana ('land of the prickly
bush'), as Amerindian settlers
called the island. Also a
comprehensive collection of
Montserrat's unusual stamps. A
treat for philatelists.
Open: Wednesday and Saturday
14.30–17.00hrs.

Eating Out
When in Wapping, look no
further than the **Emerald Café**
(tel: 809/491 3821) with its
courtyard garden, good
seafood, continental and West
Indian dishes. The **Blue
Dolphin**, Parsons (tel: 809/491
3263) is a popular local spot
where the ambience does battle
with cable TV. But for a real taste
of Montserrat head for **Mrs
Morgan's** (St John's) for the
island's best 'goat water' (stew).
More chic options include a
table on the verandah at **Belham
Valley** (tel: 809/491 5553) for
gourmet dining with a West
Indian twist; and the upmarket
Vue Pointe Hotel, Vue Pointe
(tel: 809/491 5210) holds
renowned Wednesday-night
barbecues and Sunday
brunches.

**Volcanic Activity on
Montserrat**
At the time of writing, recent
eruptions have forced the south
of the island to be evacuated.
Although volcanic ash is a
problem to the north of the
island, normal sporting activities
and excursions are still
possible. Experts are currently
monitoring the situation.

ST KITTS

Carib Indians named it
Liamuiga, the Fertile Land;
Columbus called it after
St Christopher, his namesake
and the patron saint of travellers;
and the British shortened the
name to St Kitts after establishing
their first successful Caribbean
colony here in 1623. St Kitts is
shaped like a tadpole, and it is
certainly fertile. The rainforest
heights of Mount Liamuiga
(3,792ft/1,156m), in the body of
the tadpole, give way to rolling
acres of sugar cane. The island's
arid tail, which sports the best
beaches and main tourist hotels,
trails off down to The Narrows, a
2-mile (3km) wide channel
which separates St Kitts from tiny
Nevis (see pages 36–7).

*Bathers brave the jagged Black
Rocks on the Atlantic shore*

◆
BASSETERRE

Tucked into a bay on the
southwest coast, Basseterre
dates from the days when
French colonists as well as the
British laid claim to the island.
Behind the waterfront, streets of
two-storeyed Georgian wood
and stone buildings with
gingerbread trimmings stretch
between The Circus, with its
stately Victorian clocktower, and
Independence Square. The
grassy square, bordered by
colonial townhouses, has a
fountain at the centre, and
chickens peck about in the
shade of poinciana trees. The
poinciana, which bears brilliant
red-orange blooms in July and
August, was named after a 17th-
century French governor,
Philippe de Poinci. It is the
national flower of St Kitts, and is
found throughout the Caribbean.

◆
BLACK ROCKS
northeast coast
A single coast road encircles the
island, with a spur running off
down the tail. This jagged
collection of black volcanic
rocks clawing out into the
Atlantic is a popular stop on a
round-island sightseeing tour.

◆◆
BRIMSTONE HILL FORTRESS
*22 miles (35km) northwest of
Basseterre*
After a brief period of Anglo-
French co-operation, when the
early colonists united to massacre
the Carib Indian population at
Bloody Point (a few miles north of
Basseterre) in 1626, the British
and the French fought over
St Kitts for more than a century.
British troops first fortified

Brimstone Hill, a rocky peak 800 feet (245m) above the coast, in 1690. The fortifications eventually spread over 37 acres (15ha), and the colossal fort was nicknamed the 'Gibraltar of the West Indies'. It is a stiff clamber up to the hilltop citadel with views across to neighbouring islands. Several partially restored buildings house historical background information and finds that include old clay pipes, musket balls and a smattering of Amerindian artefacts. There is a self-guided trail around battlements bristling with cannon, the former officers' quarters and ordnance store. Keep an eye out for vervet monkeys, introduced to St Kitts as pets by the French, but now something of a pest.
Open: daily, 09.30–17.30hrs.

◆◆◆
FRIAR'S BAY and FRIGATE BAY
south of Basseterre
Two of the best beaches on the island, these two strips of soft, golden sand line the leeward side of the tadpole's tail and get very busy when cruise ships are visiting. To escape the crowds, head south down to Major's Bay or Banana Bay, facing Nevis.

◆◆◆
ROMNEY MANOR
Old Road Town (northwest of Basseterre)
A modest 17th-century 'great house' (as former plantation homes are often called in the region), set in tropical gardens, Romney Manor is now occupied by **Caribelle Batik**. Most visitors come here to stock up on pretty, hand-printed

Caribbean fabrics, and watch the textile-making process. In the gardens a giant 400-year-old samaan tree spreads its bromeliad-studded branches over one-eighth of an acre (500sq m). On the road up to the Manor, look for the Amerindian rock carvings etched onto a boulder near the turn-off from the main island road.
Open: Monday to Friday 08.00–16.00hrs.

Eating Out
Right in the heart of Basseterre, **Ballahoo**, The Circus (tel: 869/465 4197) serves salads, burgers and seafood platters with veranda views; or head around the waterfront to **Ocean Terrace Inn** (tel: 869/465 2754) for fine local cuisine. Down on Frigate Bay, **The Patio** (tel: 869/465 8666) is an elegant spot; but the most delectable dining experience on the island is probably the **Rawlins Plantation** (tel: 869/465 6221), a beautifully restored plantation house hotel and restaurant at the northern end of the island.

NEVIS
A tiny volcanic blip, acting as full point to St Kitts' exclamation mark, Nevis rises steeply from the shore to a peak of 3,232 feet (985m). Columbus named her *Nuestra Señora de las Nieves* (Our Lady of the Snows), but to the prosperous 17th- and 18th-century plantation owners she was the 'Queen of the Caribbees'. Nevis (pronounced *Nee-vis*) was carpeted in sugar cane. The island had an important slave market as well as a reputation for hospitality,

which rescued Horatio Nelson from the doldrums of Antigua, and even provided him with a wife, Fanny Nisbet, whom he married here in 1787.

CHARLESTOWN

Sleepy Charlestown is strung out along a quiet main street lined with faded West Indian gingerbread buildings. At the northern end of town, **Alexander Hamilton House** was the birthplace of the 18th-century American statesman whose portrait graces US $10 bills. The ground floor has been turned into a modest local history museum with exhibits on sugar, slavery and architecture; the Nevis Assembly meets upstairs to conduct island business. *Hamilton House open*: Monday to Friday 08.00–16.00hrs; weekends in season.

♦♦♦
HORATIO NELSON MUSEUM

5 miles (8km) east of Charlestown
A riveting small museum absolutely stuffed with memorabilia pertaining to the British naval hero, Admiral Lord Nelson. Among the historical displays and paintings are scale models of HMS *Victory*, Nelson's flagship at the Battle of Trafalgar, commemorative plates and Staffordshire pottery figures. *Open*: Monday to Friday 09.00–16.00hrs; Saturday 10.00hrs–noon.

♦♦
PINNEY'S BEACH

north of Charlestown
The island's finest beach unfurls for more than 3 miles (5km)

along the shore in a swathe of golden sand from Charlestown all the way to the ruins of Fort Ashby. There are palm trees for shade, a couple of beach bars for refreshment, and watersports equipment is available for hire.

♦♦
ST JOHN'S FIG TREE CHURCH

4 miles (6.5km) east of Charlestown
A pretty country church rebuilt in 1838, St John's main claim to fame is the church register recording the marriage of Horatio Nelson to Fanny Nisbet, which took place at the nearby Montpelier Plantation. Prince William Henry, the Duke of Clarence (later King William IV), came along to give the bride away, and his signature is also recorded.

Eating Out

For cheap and cheerful local dining in Charlestown, check out **Eddy's Restaurant**, Main Street (tel: 869/469 5958); or **Unella's** (tel: 869/469 5574), on the waterfront. Nevis is famous for its gracious plantation house hotels, and most welcome non-residents for lunch or dinner. All these properties lie off the road east of Charlestown, and reservations are advisable. First up, beyond Fig Tree Village, the **Hermitage Inn** (tel: 869/469 3477) serves lunch and dinner on a pretty terrace extending from the antique-filled, 18th-century house. The elegantly informal **Montpelier Plantation Inn** (tel: 869/469 3462) is set in lovely gardens. After lunch at the **Golden Rock Estate** (tel: 869/ 469 3346), there are rainforest walking trails to explore.

THE VIRGIN ISLANDS

The Virgin Islands lie scattered across 1,000 square miles (2,600sq km) of dazzling turquoise sea on the northeastern rim of the Caribbean. There are around 100 bite-sized volcanic islands, cays, reefs and rocks divided between the more developed US Virgin Islands (USVI) to the west (see pages 42–6), and the quieter, magnificently laid-back British Virgin Islands (BVI), a British Crown Colony.

BRITISH VIRGIN ISLANDS

Columbus sailed through the islands in 1493, and named them after the 11,000 beautiful virgins in the legend of St Ursula. Sir Francis Drake also navigated his way through the tricky channels and shoals in 1585; the Sir Francis Drake Channel, carving a route through the BVI, is one of the most picturesque seagoing experiences in the world. Pirates and privateers found the islands' hidden coves and bays ideal. Today, these same secluded inlets now attract pleasure-seeking yachtsmen and the Virgin Islands are recognised as one of the world's most desirable sailing destinations. This is Robinson-Crusoe-with-a-gold-card territory, with a smattering of luxurious, but low-key hotels (nothing taller than a palm tree) providing elegant accommodation, fine dining and gourmet picnics to order. Despite the islands' proximity to the Americanised bustle of the USVI, life in the BVI is infinitely slower and more friendly.

TORTOLA

On the north side of the Sir Francis Drake Channel, Tortola is the largest island in the BVI, measuring just 11 miles by 3 miles (17km by 5km). It was named after the turtle doves which still outnumber the small, scrubby island's 15,000 inhabitants, most of whom live in the capital and cruise ship berth of Road Town.

◆
ROAD TOWN

A mere handful of small streets
behind a broad bay, Road Town
has few pretentions, but offers a
small selection of souvenir and
crafts shops on Main Street, a
jovial pub, and an historical
museum with mysterious
opening hours. A reasonable
stroll to the east of the town
centre, the **J R O'Neal Botanic**

*Shopping, yachting and dining in
Tortola's West End*

Gardens make a pleasant
detour. Established in 1986, the
gardens have flourished with a
waterlily pond, orchid house
and wooden benches set amid a
riot of bougainvillaea and
shaded by palm trees.
Botanic Gardens open: daily,
dawn to dusk.

CANE GARDEN BAY
north coast
This lovely sandy strand lies over the hill from Road Town, with a couple of hotels set back from the beach. There are windsurfers and dinghies for hire, waterskiing, and beach bars with views to the neighbouring islands. Across the road, among the mossy boulders and rusting remains of sugar boiling pans, the **Callwood Rum Distillery** still produces the local brew in the old fashioned way.

SAGE MOUNTAIN NATIONAL PARK
southwest of Road Town
The highest point on the island (1,780ft/542m), Mount Sage commands fabulous views out across the BVI. Trails plunge into the primeval rainforest, edged by giant ferns and glossy elephant-ear vines, wild guava and 100-foot- (30m) high bulletwood trees.

◆◆
WEST END
The main hotels are tucked away at Tortola's western end, with easy access to the island's best beaches on the north coast. Ferries to Jost van Dyke and Virgin Gorda (BVI), St Thomas and St John (USVI), depart from **Soper's Hole**, an attractive marina and waterfront shopping complex, which makes a good lunch stop.

Eating Out
Facing the waterfront in Road Town, **Pusser's Outpost** (tel: 809/494 4199) offers a broad menu of snacks, pub grub and more substantial fare. Fun-loving yachtsmen tend to gravitate towards the lively **Last Resort**, Trellis Bay (tel: 809/495 2520), a bar-restaurant with entertainment on Beef Island. The charming, colonial-style **Sugar Mill Hotel**, Apple Bay (tel: 809/495 4355) has a lovely restaurant serving gourmet West Indian dishes. On Cane Garden Bay, **Quito's Gazebo** (tel: 809/495 4837) is renowned for seafood; for local food without the frills, check out **Mrs Scatliffe's** (tel: 809/495 4556).

JOST VAN DYKE
A stone's throw north of Tortola, the tiny island of Jost van Dyke makes a great away-day escape with beautiful beaches and little in the way of tourist facilities. The island was named for a Dutch pirate who would probably have thoroughly enjoyed the massive New Year's party celebrated annually on the beach, when some 2,000 revellers descend for the night, then disappear to nurse their sore heads and leave the islanders to sleep it off until next year.

Visitors arrive at the grandly-named **Great Harbour**, a picturesque collection of faded West Indian houses on the bay. The most popular beach is dazzling **White Bay**, to the west.

Eating Out
Foxy's, Great Bay (tel: 809/495 9258) is *the* place to hang out on Jost van Dyke. The liveliest of several beach bars, it serves cold beers, cocktails and simple food.

◆◆◆
VIRGIN GORDA ✓

A 5-mile (8km) hop east of
Tortola, the 'fat virgin' (so named
because Columbus, who may
have been on the grog, thought
it resembled a pregnant woman
reclining), is the most exclusive
corner of the BVI. Laurance
Rockefeller established the Little
Dix Bay hotel on the 8-square
mile (20sq km) island in the
1960s, since when the equally
understated but luxurious Biras
Creek and Bitter End Yacht Club
resorts have joined the fray.
Ferries from Tortola put in at
Spanish Town, on the southwest
coast, close to the island's best
beaches. Near by, Virgin
Gorda's number one tourist
attraction is **The Baths**, an
imposing jumble of massive
granite boulders, caves and
grottoes tipping towards the
shore. This freakish collection of
rocks has puzzled scientists for
years as its nearest geological
relations are found in the
Carolinas several thousand
miles away.
The Baths tends to be the only
place on the island which ever
gets crowded. To escape the
sightseers, take a 15-minute
hike south along a nature trail to
the secluded coral sand shore at
Devil's Bay National Park; or
head inland and hike **Gorda
Peak** (1,358ft/414m), the island's
highest point.
Gun Creek, the second largest
settlement on Virgin Gorda,
overlooks the yachts and
beaches of beautiful **North
Sound**. This is the place to catch
a boat to Biras Creek or the
Bitter End Yacht Club.

The Baths, Virgin Gorda

Eating Out
The **Olde Yard Inn**, The Valley
(tel: 809/495 5544) is a friendly
and reasonably priced spot
serving local and international
dishes; as is **Pusser's** (tel:
809/495 7369), a nautical-style
pub on Leverick Bay. Out on the
islands in North Sound, **Pirate's
Pub**, Saba Rock (tel: 809/495
9638) is a rollicking dive for
passing yachties; while **Drake's
Anchorage**, Prickly Pear Cay
(tel: 809/494 2254) has scenic
views and good seafood dishes.
The **Biras Creek Hotel** (tel:
809/494 3555) is probably the
chief gourmet haunt on the
island. Its closest non-hotel rival
is **Chez Michelle**, The Valley
(tel: 809/495 5510).

US VIRGIN ISLANDS

It's official: this is the 'American Paradise', or so it says on local car licence plates. To the east of Puerto Rico, bustling, fully Americanised St Thomas, and neighbouring St John, which is for the most part a national park, are the two most visited of the USVI. Some 40 miles (65km) to the south, St Croix is quieter and less pretty, but offers more in the way of sightseeing.

The Danish West Indies Company claimed St Thomas and St John in the late 17th century, when they set up trading posts and plantations growing sugar cane, cotton and indigo. St Croix was purchased from the French in 1733, and the freeport of St Thomas profited hugely during the American War of Independence. After the collapse of the sugar trade in the early 20th century, the Danes sold their Caribbean colonies to the US for $25 million, and the rest, as they say, is history.

ST CROIX

Well to the south of the main archipelago, St Croix (pronounced *Croy*) is the largest of the Virgin Islands at 82 square miles (212sq km). The island's fertile lowlands proved good sugar-growing country during the plantation era, and it jockeyed for position with St Thomas until pretty St Thomas cornered the tourist market in the 1960s. But St Croix gained an oil refinery, and both islands are now among the richest and most developed in the region. St Croix, however,

Spectacular sunning and snorkelling at Trunk Bay, St John

ticks over at a slower pace, and the good-natured locals always have time to stop for a chat.

◆◆
CHRISTIANSTED

The Danish influence is alive and well in the island capital laid out in 1733, and named in honour of King Christian VI. The sheltered port is guarded by decorative Fort Christiansvaern, and attractive shopping streets lead back from the waterfront lined with arcaded stone buildings dating from the 18th and 19th centuries.

A stroll around the battlements of **Fort Christiansvaern** is a must. The pristine little yellow-and-white fort, largely built between 1738 and 1749, bristles with cannon backed up by neat pyramids of cannon balls. It looks more suited to toy soldiers than the real thing, and indeed the fort never fired a shot in anger.
Fort Christiansvaern open: Monday to Friday 09.00–17.00hrs.

◆◆◆
BUCK ISLAND NATIONAL PARK

St Croix's best beach is actually a couple of miles offshore on Buck Island. There are frequent boat departures (one hour) from Christiansted, and the 850-acre (345ha) park has picnicking facilities as well as two underwater trails offering excellent snorkelling.

Just a couple of minutes from the Christiansted waterfront (also served by ferry), **Protestant Cay** is another beach option. On the mainland, try **Buccaneer Beach**, **Chenay Bay**, or **Cramer Park** among others.

◆
FREDERIKSTED

Cruise ships can arrive at either Christiansted or the island's second town, small and sleepy Frederiksted, a 30-minute drive away on the west coast. On the harbour, **Fort Frederik** dates from 1752, and houses a well-laid out island history museum with interesting sections on local culture and hurricanes. St Croix was devastated by Hurricane Hugo in 1989, which left around 90 per cent of the population homeless, though most of the damage has since been repaired.

Facing the waterfront, in a row of old 'skirt-and-blouse' style buildings (stone ground floors and wooden upper stories decorated with gingerbread detail), there are a few shops and restaurants, plus the small but fascinating **St Croix Aquarium**. Some 20 tanks reveal all sorts of strange and frequently beautiful creatures, from shimmering reef fish to dentist shrimps who spend their lives paddling about the seabed cleaning other creatures' teeth. *Fort Frederik open*: Monday to Friday 08.30–16.00hrs. *Aquarium open*: Wednesday to Sunday 11.00–16.00hrs.

◆
ST GEORGE VILLAGE BOTANICAL GARDEN
Centerline Road
Arawak Indians once made camp on this 16-acre (6.5ha) site east of Frederiksted. The attractive lawned gardens are laid out around the ruins of an old sugar mill and contain over 800 species of tropical plants bordering a trail with a rainforest section and scented frangipani walk.
Open: Tuesday to Saturday 09.00–16.00hrs.

◆◆◆
WHIM GREAT HOUSE
Centerline Road
A splendidly restored 18th-century plantation house, Whim is something of a curiosity with its unusual oval-shaped interior. The rooms have been furnished with period antiques and paintings, and the 3-foot- (1m) thick walls and air moat keep it refreshingly cool. The old sugar mill and cane crushers are on view in the grounds.
Open: Monday to Saturday 10.00–17.00hrs.

Eating Out
Downtown Christiansted offers numerous good restaurants and bistros. There is patio dining and pasta at **Dino's**, 4-C Hospital Street (tel: 809/778 8005); seafood and local cuisine at the relaxed **Club Comanche**, 1 Strand Street (tel: 809/773 2665); and Danish specialities at the elegant **Top Hat**, 52 Company Street (tel: 809/773 2346). In Frederiksted, chill out with Cajun cooking and jazz at **Blue Moon** (tel: 809/772 2222), under the arches on Front Street.

ST JOHN
Two-thirds of the island of St John is maintained, or rather left alone to do its own thing, by the US National Parks Service. Donated by Laurance Rockefeller in 1956, this rare 12,900-acre (7,775ha) pocket of undeveloped terrain lies a breezy 30-minute boat ride from St Thomas. Ferries put in at Cruz Bay, near the Mongoose Junction information centre (tel: 809/776 6201), where visitors can pick up trail guides, camping details and schedules for ranger-led walks, wildlife lectures and other activities.
The hilly backcountry has mostly reverted to forest tumbling down to a series of gorgeous north coast beaches. The most famous is **Trunk Bay**, rated among National Geographic's top ten beaches in the world, with a coral reef snorkelling trail. **Cruz Bay**, to the west, is the most developed

corner of the island with several hotels, restaurants and bars, and a local history museum. Overlooking the north coast at the end of the road, the 18th-century **Annaberg Plantation** ruins are a popular stop with terrific views across to the neighbouring islands. Several days a week there are short guided tours around the old mill buildings.

Eating Out

Cruz Bay's hotels provide the most upmarket dining on St John, but for a lovely setting in an old wooden house, the **Old Gallery** (tel: 809/776 7544) serves classic West Indian dishes and more international fare. Near by, there is seafood at the **Fish Trap**; or health foods and binge-worthy ice creams at **Luscious Licks** on Main Street. At the eastern end of the island, **Shipwreck Landing**, Coral Bay (tel: 809/776 8640) is a cheap and cheerful local spot with a garden above the waterfront.

Historic Charlotte Amalie

ST THOMAS

St Thomas is the administrative centre of the USVI, and its number one tourist attraction. Some 50,000 people inhabit the green-cloaked 12½-mile by 3-mile (20km by 5km) volcanic island, and their numbers are boosted daily by a steady flow of cruise passengers disgorged onto the wharf at Charlotte Amalie.

◆◆◆
CHARLOTTE AMALIE

The first settlement on Charlotte Amalie's beautiful bay was known as 'Taphus' ('taphouse'), and since its early days the port has been an important trading centre and favoured watering hole for visitors to the region. The Danes renamed it in honour of Queen Charlotte Amalie in 1691, and in 1724 St Thomas was declared a free port, which it has remained ever since. Charlotte Amalie's famous shopping action is concentrated between Main Street and the

waterfront, where more than 400 shops and stores are piled high with gifts and souvenirs, designer fashions and jewellery. On the sightseeing front, take a look around the island history displays laid out in **Fort Christian**, the harbour fortress founded in 1672.

Behind the busy waterfront, Charlotte Amalie climbs steeply uphill in a cat's-cradle of pretty pastel houses, 19th-century public buildings and narrow, shady streets linked by flights of steps. The so-called 99 Steps (actually there are 103) scale the hill to **Blackbeard's Tower**, a stone lookout where the infamous pirate is said to have taken refuge and kept watch for potential victims.

ATLANTIS SUBMARINES
Havensight Mall

The perfect way to reef dive without getting your hair wet, these mini-submarine adventures are so popular it is advisable to book in advance (tel: 809/776 5650). The one-hour dive reaches depths of 90 feet (27m), and there are terrific views of corals and marine life around the Buck Island Reef.
Open: Monday to Saturday 09.00–15.00hrs.

CORAL WORLD MARINE PARK AND UNDERWATER OBSERVATORY
Coki Beach (northeast)

A land-based opportunity to come face to face with bizarre and brilliant marine creatures and corals on show in an 80,000-gallon (365,000-litre) reef tank.

There is also an underwater observatory, shark and fish feeding demonstrations, and convenient changing facilities for visitors to adjacent Coki Beach.
Open: daily, 09.00–17.00hrs.

DRAKE'S SEAT
Skyline Drive

A scenic drive up into the central highlands passes the Drake's Seat lookout, where English naval hero Sir Francis Drake is supposed to have kept an eye on the Spanish fleet.

MAGENS BAY
Magens Road (north coast)

St Thomas' most stunning beach (and another contender in National Geographic's top ten beaches of the world, along with Trunk Bay on St John), Magens Bay is a tropical idyll. The mile-long crescent of powder-soft sand curves around the bay fringed by palm trees.

Eating Out

For good food and a marvellous setting in Charlotte Amalie, the historic **Hotel 1829**, Government Hill (tel: 809/776 1234) would be hard to beat. A good local spot with courtyard dining is **Gladys' Café**, behind 17 Main Street (tel: 809/774 6604). To the west of the town centre in Frenchtown, **Café Normandie** (tel: 809/774 1622) is very elegant, and very French; while **Alexander's Café** (tel: 809/774 4349) serves seafood, pasta and Austrian specials (the affiliated **Bar & Grill** is more reasonable).

THE LESSER ANTILLES

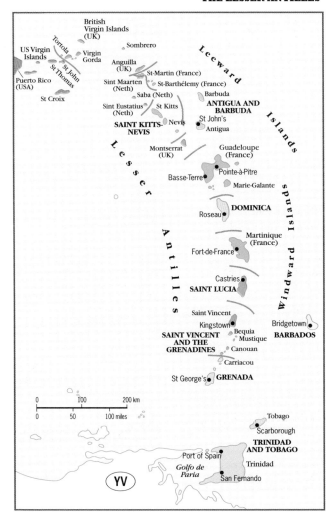

THE FRENCH ANTILLES

The French Antilles spread over a distance of 350 miles (560km), from the Leeward Island territories of St Bartélemy (see pages 56–7) and Saint-Martin (see pages 68–9), down to Guadeloupe and Martinique in the Windwards. The islands' French influence is unmistakable in everything from road signs and *croissants* to games of *boules* played on shady squares. But the true spirit of the French Antilles is Creole, a zesty French-African enjoyment of life, good food and beautiful women.

GUADELOUPE

An exotic butterfly shape, Guadeloupe is actually two islands pushed together by seismic upheaval and linked by a bridge. The mountainous western wing, Basse-Terre, contains the towering Soufrière volcano (4,813ft/1,467m), the highest point in the eastern Caribbean. Grande-Terre, the eastern wing, is a rolling limestone plateau fringed with beaches and well developed for tourism.

Guadeloupe's contrasting wings have equally diverse chief towns. Although the sleepy town of Basse-Terre is the island's administrative capital, the commercial centre of Pointe-à-Pitre, in the southwest corner of Grande-Terre, is far larger and the main entry point for air and cruise ship passengers.

◆
BASSE-TERRE

Crouched in the lee of La Soufrière on the southwest coast, the dozy island capital still retains a portion of its colonial charm and stone and wood buildings. The town was founded in 1643, a few years before construction began on the massive bulwark of **Fort St Charles**, which guards the harbour and now houses a small museum.

◆◆
POINTE-À-PITRE

Guadeloupe's frenetic main port is no Caribbean beauty. Behind the sprawling waterfront market stalls on La Darse (the harbour), the streets are narrow and congested with far too many ugly concrete buildings to be described as picturesque. However, there are pockets of native charm such as the gardens of the **Place de la Victoire**, edged by distinctly Gallic cafés and a handful of old colonial houses. A small flower market brightens up the square outside the **Cathedral of St Peter and St Paul**, and the covered market, on rue Frébault, is an entertaining collection of stalls piled high with fruit and vegetables, spices and basketware overseen by voluble matrons.

On rue Peynier, the **Musée Schoelcher** occupies a pretty French townhouse. It honours the 19th-century abolitionist, Victor Schoelcher, who championed the anti-slavery movement, and displays mementoes of the great man together with assorted plantation era artefacts and paintings.

To the south of town, **Bas du Fort's** popular marina has several restaurants. Further

The dramatic cascades of the Chutes du Carbet in Guadeloupe's Parc National

along the road to Le Gosier, the **Aquarium de la Guadeloupe** showcases strange and exotic tropical fish.

Musée Schoelcher open: Monday to Friday 09.00hrs–noon and 14.30–17.30hrs.

Aquarium de la Guadeloupe open: daily, 09.00–1900hrs.

◆◆◆
CHUTES DU CARBET

near St-Sauveur, Basse-Terre

A dramatic climb from the village of St-Sauveur and the coast road, these popular waterfalls plummet down the mountainside in three stages. The most impressive is the second spill, a 360-foot (110m) cascade, which can be reached by a 20-minute trek through the rainforest.

Downtown Basse-Terre

◆◆◆
GRANDE-TERRE

Grande-Terre gets top marks for beaches. Closest to Pointe-à-Pitre on the south coast, the resort towns of **Le Gosier**, **Ste-Anne** and **St-François** are popular and often crowded. For something rather more off the beaten track, try the secluded west coast beaches of **Morne à l'Eau** or **Anse du Souffle**; or head north to **La Porte d'Enfer**. Between Pointe-à-Pitre and Le Gosier, **Fort Fleur d'Épée** is worth a short detour for the views. The 18th-century coral rock ruins make a grand lookout down the coast of Basse-Terre to Pointe Capesterre and across to the island of Marie-Galante.
Fort Fleur d'Épée open: daily, 09.00–18.00hrs.

◆
MAISON DU BOIS
south of Pointe Noire, Basse-Terre
An interesting quick stop on a round-island tour, the 'House of Wood' exhibits antique tools, domestic utensils and island furniture from lobster pots and coffee grinders to a grandiose 19th-century bed. Artisans from the woodcraft centre of Pointe Noire also come to sell their handicrafts here.
Open: daily, 09.15–17.00hrs.

◆◆
MAISON DU VOLCAN
St-Claude, Bassse-Terre
The somewhat precipitous road to St-Claude cuts up behind Basse-Terre and the temperature drops appreciably as you reach this beautifully positioned old planters' quarter with its attractive Creole houses and tropical gardens. The Maison du Volcan augments general exhibits about vulcanism in the Caribbean with specific data on the volcano La Soufrière and its eruption in 1976.
Near by, the village of **Matouba** is famous for its hot springs which bubble up from the ground at a constant 138°F (59°C).
Open: daily, 10.00–18.00hrs.

◆
MUSÉE DU RHUM
Ste-Rose, Basse-Terre
A chance to sample Guadeloupean rum straight from the manufacturer. Tastings are prefaced by displays and a short film covering every last detail of the distilling process.
Open: Monday to Saturday 09.00–17.00hrs; Sunday 10.00–13.00hrs and 15.00–17.00hrs.

◆◆◆
PARC NATIONAL DE LA GUADELOUPE ✓

Route de la Traversée, Basse-Terre
The Carib Indians named Guadeloupe *Karukera* ('Island of Beautiful Waters'), and it lives up to this name in the magnificent national park that encompasses some 74,000 acres (30,000ha) of rainforest highlands stretching down to La Soufrière. The Route de la Traversée literally traverses Basse-Terre from east to west carving its way up through exuberant rainforest vegetation and across the Col des Mamelles (The Breasts), a 2,500-foot- (760m) high pass between twin volcanic peaks. To the east, the **Cascade aux Écrevisses** is a waterfall picnic spot in the foothills. It is cool here under the forest canopy, and visitors find it hard to resist scrambling around the mossy boulders at the water's edge. A few miles further on, the **Maison de la Forêt** is the place to pick up information and walking guides to the park's 190-mile (300km) network of marked paths and forest trails. On the Caribbean coast, the underwater **Réserve Naturelle de Pigeon** has been nicknamed the 'Reserve Cousteau' after the world-famous French oceanographer who supported a ban on deep-sea fishing around tiny Pigeon Island. Glass-bottomed boats make frequent forays over the island's stunning coral reefs.
Maison de la Forêt open: daily, 09.00–17.00hrs.

◆◆
LA SOUFRIÈRE
hiking access from Savane à Mulets, Basse-Terre
A narrow road continues east from St-Claude and the Maison du Volcan (see page 50) to Savane à Mulets, 1,000 feet (300m) below Soufrière's summit. The volcano has been relatively quiet since 1976, and several well-marked trails strike off up to its sulphurous summit craters where boiling mud pools and steaming fumaroles bubble and hiss in the unearthly landscape. The uphill hike to the top takes around two hours.

Eating Out
At the foot of the gangplank in Pointe-à-Pitre, **La Canne à Sucre**, Centre St-John Perse (tel: 590/82 10 19) is one of Guadeloupe's top dining experiences, serving French and inventive island cuisine. Grande-Terre's south coast resorts are well-supplied with waterfront restaurants and bistros such as **Le Mérou d'Or**, Le Gosier (tel: 590/84 02 27), which specialises in fish dishes. In the northeast, **Château de Feuilles**, Anse Bertrand (tel: 590/22 30 30) accompanies French cuisine with a choice of 25 fruit-flavoured rums.

MARTINIQUE

Carib Indians called it *Madinina*, the Island of Flowers, and Martinique is still renowned for its flora, as well as for fine beaches and beautiful women. When French settlers finally ousted the Caribs in the 1630s, they planted sugar cane, and Martinique prospered to become the most important of the French possessions in the Caribbean. Its once elegant commercial centre, St-Pierre, was known as the Paris of the Antilles.

Northern Martinique rises up through lush, green *mornes* (foothills) to the peak of Mont Pelée (4,583ft/1397m), which erupted in 1902, destroying St-Pierre. Midway down the leeward coast, Fort-de-France is the island's administrative seat and chief port. The southern portion of Martinique is

Vibrant Haïtian art on sale in Fort-de-France

carpeted with rippling sugar cane fields, and the best beaches are found here together with the main tourist centres.

◆
FORT-DE-FRANCE

A major city by Caribbean standards, Martinique's vibrant capital has over 100,000 inhabitants living in the waterfront city centre and suburbs spread out around the encircling hills. The harbour on Baie des Flamands is guarded by **Fort St-Louis**, founded on the point in 1639, and still occupied by the military. Near by, ferry boats (*vedettes*) make regular departures for the bayside beaches of Pointe du Bout, Anse Mitan, and Anse-à-l'Ane.

Behind the waterfront, the 12-acre (5ha) **La Savane gardens** provide a welcome breathing space with walkways and flowerbeds beneath huge palm trees. Overlooking the gardens, on rue de la Liberté, the **Musée Départemental** displays a notable collection of Amerindian artefacts; and the splendidly bizarre **Bibliothèque Schoelcher** was designed for the 1889 Paris Exposition.

The main shopping district, extending north from rue de la Liberté, is the place to splash out on French luxury items, and inspect the stained-glass windows in the **Cathédrale St-Louis**. On the edge of the city centre, the **Parc Floral** is a mass of blooms, with a botanical and geological gallery in the grounds.

Musée Départemental open: Monday to Friday 09.00–17.00hrs; Saturday 09.00hrs–noon.

AJOUPA-BOUILLON
northeast of St-Pierre
In the lee of Mont Pelée, this pretty flower-bedecked village is the starting point for trails up through the forest to the **Gorges de la Falaise**, narrow gorges hollowed out of the rock by the Falaise river. For a less taxing stroll, follow the botanic trail through the rainforest from Les Ombrages, just below town.

JARDIN DE BALATA
route de la Trace, 5 miles (8km) north of Fort-de-France
Perched in the hills above the city, these glorious gardens are a mass of brilliant bougainvillaea, hibiscus, ginger plants, heliconias, flamboyant (royal poinciana) trees and other tropical species. Humming birds put on a dazzling display of speed and grace as they zip from bloom to bloom dipping their curved bills into the nectar-rich recesses. There are shady areas where anthuriums and bromeliads flourish, and winding paths offer views over plunging ravines in the forest.
Open: daily, 09.00–17.00hrs.

MUSÉE GAUGUIN
Anse Turin, south of St-Pierre
In 1887, the French painter Paul Gauguin set sail to find a tropical paradise where he could live as a 'noble savage'. When Panama proved too developed, he ended up on the beach in Martinique, where he spent five months. It was not a success, and this small museum displays copies of disconsolate letters written to his wife alongside reproductions of his paintings.
Open: daily, 09.30–17.30hrs.

MUSÉE DE LA PAGERIE
near Les Trois-Ilets, 16 miles (25km) south of Fort-de-France
Napoleon Bonaparte's wife, the Empress Josephine, was born on the sugar plantation estate that once stood in this pretty valley. A few ruins survive, and a single-roomed stone cottage now houses memorabilia of Marie-Rose Joséphine Tascher de la Pagerie's Caribbean

childhood, paintings, documents and letters from the future French Emperor.
Open: Tuesday to Sunday 09.00–17.00hrs.

◆◆
POINTE DU BOUT and LES TROIS-ILETS
southwest of Fort-de-France
Pointe du Bout is one of the busiest resort areas on the island with a selection of hotels, restaurants and shops backing the beach. There is watersports equipment for hire, and yacht charters from the marina.
For a complete change of pace, the road runs south through the cane fields to the pretty fishing village of Les Trois-Ilets which hosts a Saturday morning market on the tiny square. *En route*, the **Maison de la Canne**, a museum of sugar cane, makes an interesting stop. Its informative plantation era exhibits include a wooden cane-crushing mill and a rum distillery.
Maison de la Canne open: Tuesday to Sunday 09.00–17.00hrs.

◆◆
ROCHER DU DIAMANT (DIAMOND ROCK)
Pointe du Diamant (south coast)
A huge, sheer-sided rock about a mile (1.6km) from the shore, the Diamond was once commissioned as a British naval 'battleship'. In 1804, a garrison was established on HMS *Diamond Rock*, as it was known, to irritate the Martiniquans. It held out for 18 months, hoisting supplies from visiting ships below, until the French initiated

a three-day bombardment and sent the occupiers packing.

◆
SACRÉ-COEUR
route de la Trace
A popular stop near the Jardin de Balata, the 'Montmartre martiniquais' is a scaled-down replica, constructed in 1923, of the famous basilica church in Paris. There are fine views over the city.

◆◆
ST-PIERRE
northwest coast
After several days of advance rumblings, largely ignored by the 25,000 inhabitants of St-Pierre, Mont Pelée erupted at 08.00hrs on 8 May 1902. Within minutes a cloud of poisonous gas and burning ash swept over the town, killing the entire

Above Fort-de-France, the Martiniquan Sacré-Coeur was built as a World War I memorial

30,000-strong population with
the exception of a drunk locked
up in an underground cell.
The town never recovered,
though a small village has
sprung up around the ominous
ruins. There are miniature train
tours, and the ghoulish before-
and-after story of the fatal
eruption is told in the **Musée
Vulcanologique**. Among the
melted glassware and fused
musket balls are sepia
photographs of St-Pierre before
the eruption.
Musée Vulcanologique open:
daily, 09.00hrs–noon and
15.00–17.00hrs.

STE-ANNE
south coast
Down on the arid south coast
peninsula, Ste-Anne is the
jumping off point for the finest
beaches on the island. There
are a number of small sandy
coves (*anses*), and the
magnificent sweep of **Les
Salines** on the southern tip of
the island. Here the desert-like
Sarane des Pétrifications
stretches off beyond the salt
pans in a barren expanse of
doughty jasper plants and
petrified wood.

TROIS RIVIÈRES RUM
DISTILLERY
east of Diamant
The national drink of the French
Antilles is *ti-punch* (white rum,
sugar cane syrup and a squeeze
of lemon), and this sugar mill-
cum-rum distillery invites
visitors to watch rum in the
making with the added
inducement of tastings.

Open: Monday to Friday
09.00hrs–noon and
14.30–17.00hrs.

Eating Out
A convenient hotel dining room
right in the heart of Fort-de-
France, **Le Lafayette**, rue de la
Liberté (tel: 596/63 24 09)
offers fine Creole food; there
are cheap and cheerful
vegetarian specials and fresh
fruit juices at **Le Second
Souffle**, rue Blénac; bistro
dishes at **Chez Gaston**, rue
Félix Eboué (tel: 596/71 45 48);
or dine out in *haute cuisine*
style at **La Mouïna**, route de la
Redoute (tel: 596/64 28 70),
perched high above the city in
an old Creole villa. Near Pointe
du Bout, **Villa Créole**, Anse
Mitan (tel: 596/66 05 53) serves
French Creole cuisine on the
terrace. Way down at the
southern beaches, sample
delicious fresh-caught seafood
at **Poi et Virginie**, Ste-Anne
(tel: 596/76 72 22).

Creole Cooking
An inspired combination of
French culinary *élan* and
Caribbean ingredients from
fresh fish to exotic fruits, Creole
cooking is one of the great
reasons to stop off in the French
Antilles. Don't miss out on a *blaff*
(fish or lobster cooked in
spices), or *crabes farcis* (stuffed
crabs with herbs), and some of
the best *accras* (battered spicy
fish balls) are served by stalls
on the waterfront. *Colombo* is a
traditional curry; *lambi* (conch
tenderised with lime) is popular
in salads, chowders and fritters;
and fried plantain often appear
as vegetables.

THE FRENCH ANTILLES

ST-BARTHÉLEMY

Chic St-Barthélemy (better known as St Barts) is probably the most expensive and exclusive outpost in the Caribbean. It is indisputably French, and the boutiques of the capital, Gustavia, are piled high with designer goodies from couture frocks to champagne, cognac and Chanel perfume. St Barts attracts the rich and famous like a magnet. It is also a favourite with the international yachting fraternity, who compete in December's Route de la Rose. The winner is the first 65-foot (20m) yacht over the line in Gustavia with a case of rosé wine carried across the Atlantic from the summer yachting haunt of St-Tropez. Christopher Columbus named the tiny (8-square mile/20sq km) island after his brother, Bartolomeo back in the 15th century, but St Barts was not settled until 1648. Breton sailors were the earliest colonists and they made a precarious living on the dry, scrubby island trading with pirates and smugglers. From 1785, when the French handed St Barts to Sweden in exchange for trading rights in the Baltic, the island prospered as a commercial trading post for almost a century. The free port status conferred on it by the Swedes remained intact after the French reclaimed St Barts in 1878, and the island is now a miniature duty-free gold mine.

◆◆
GUSTAVIA

The island's picturesque port capital was christened in honour of the Swedish king, Gustav III. It is only a couple of streets in total set out around three sides of the busy harbour. Four forts once stood guard over the waterfront. **Fort Oscar** is still occupied by the military, so out of bounds to curious visitors, but **Fort Gustave** has been partially restored, allowing tours of the powder magazine and kitchens. An orientation map details the neighbouring islands on view from the old battlements. Shopping in Gustavia is not recommended for the budget-conscious. Alternative distractions include drinking in the atmosphere (few bargains here either) from any number of attractive cafés and restaurants. The **Musée de St-Barth**, on the west side of the harbour, houses local history, fauna and flora exhibits.

Musée de St-Barth open: Monday to Friday 08.00–11.30hrs and 15.00–17.30hrs; Saturday 15.00–17.30hrs.

◆◆◆
COROSSOL

north of Gustavia

This charming fishing village also doubles as chief guardian of the island's cultural traditions, and it is not unusual to see the elderly ladies of Corossol sporting old-fashioned Breton bonnets (*calèches*) as they sit in the shade weaving baskets and hats from the leaves of the latanier palm.

While here, conchologists should not miss the seashell collection housed at the **Inter-Ocean Museum**, where staff are happy to help identify finds from the island's best shelling beach, **Petit Anse à Galets**, near Gustavia.

Inter-Ocean Museum open:
Tuesday to Sunday
08.00hrs–noon and
13.30–17.00hrs.

GRAND CUL-DE-SAC and PETIT CUL-DE-SAC
northeast coast
Two popular beaches flanking
either side of a small peninsula
and protected by coral reefs.
There is good swimming and
watersports equipment for hire,
plus a couple of hotels and
restaurants.

ST-JEAN
north coast
A busy beachfront development
close to the airport with all the
tourist trimmings from

*Palatial yachts jostle for position
in the exclusive confines of
Gustavia Harbour*

watersports and bistros to the
island's only shopping centre.

Eating Out
In the heart of Gustavia, **Bar Le
Select** is the social hub of the
entire island and serves food as
well as *ti-punch* cocktails; the
terrace at **Le Sapotillier** (tel:
590/27 60 28) is a lovely
gourmet haunt. **Pelican** serves
up cocktails and live music in
St-Jean; for good seafood, salads
and grills, try **Chez Francine**
(tel: 590/27 60 49). Over in
Grand Cul-de-Sac, the deluxe
Guanahani hotel (tel: 590/27 66
60) is renowned for first-class
French cuisine.

NETHERLANDS ANTILLES

Steeped in tradition: Dutch gables in Oranjestad, Aruba

Three and a half centuries of Dutch rule has left a firm imprint on the Netherlands Antilles, a total of four-and-a-half islands, plus Aruba, which was granted autonomy in 1986. Geographically, they are divided into the Dutch Leewards, or ABC Islands (Aruba, Bonaire and Curaçao) off the Venezuelan coast; and the Dutch Windwards, or SSS Islands (Saba, St Eustatius and the Dutch half of Sint Maarten/Saint-Martin), 500 miles (800km) to the north.

The local currency is a version of the Dutch guilder, and Aruba and Curaçao are noted for their picturesque pastel-painted and Dutch-gabled buildings. In the ABC Islands, Dutch and English are widely spoken, but many locals prefer to converse in Papiamento. This exotic (and incomprehensible) dialect, combining elements of Spanish, Portugese, French, Dutch, various African languages and English, was developed as a sort of international pidgin by foreign merchants and slaves during the colonial era. The SSS Islands tend to stick to English along with their Leeward Island neighbours.

ARUBA

It is thought Aruba was first sighted by Alonso de Ojeda in 1499, and claimed for Spain. However, the early colonists declared it an *isla inútil* (useless island), and the dry, scrubby 20-mile by 6-mile (32km by 10km) island was not permanently settled for more than a century. Aruba is one of the few places where native Amerindians survived the invasion of European colonists, and their distinctive features can still be seen in the faces of local people.

Aruba's early 20th-century prosperity was founded on oil, but since the 1980s, the island has capitalised on its fabulous beaches which are well-developed for tourism.

ORANJESTAD

Aruba's capital is an important cruise ship destination, its waterfront shopping malls and main street, Nassaustraat, inundated with cruising bargain hunters. Behind the mercantile frenzy, the old town of Oranjestad (pronounced *Oran-yeh-stat*) offers original Dutch Colonial-style buildings on Wilhelminastraat, and a couple of local history museums housed in and around **Fort Zoutman**, the island's oldest building, which has guarded the harbour since its completion in 1796. Laid out in the fort complex, artefacts in the **Museo Arubano** trace Aruba's chequered history from pre-colonial times up to the present day. Near by, the **Museo Archaeologico**, Zoutmanstraat 1, harks back to the very earliest days of human habitation on the island.

Museo Arubano open: Monday to Friday 09.00–16.00hrs; Saturday 09.00hrs–noon.
Museo Archaeologico open: Monday to Friday 08.00hrs–noon and 13.30–16.30hrs.

EAGLE BEACH and PALM BEACH

northwest of Oranjestad
Aruba's two finest beaches are nicknamed the 'low-rise strip' and 'high-rise strip' respectively. Hotels line the shore and offer a full range of watersports, parasailing and sail boats. The windsurfing conditions are excellent, and competitions are held here in summer. Deep-sea fishing charters can be arranged, as well as dive trips and sunset cruises.

HOOIBERG

central (east of Oranjestad)
After a wander around the tropical Indian Rock Garden at the foot of the Hooiberg (Haystack Hill), visitors can scale the modest heights of Aruba's 541-foot (165m) mini-mountain with the help of a staircase carved into the rock. Views stretch out across the arid, cactus-dotted backcountry which the locals call the *cunucu*. A short distance northeast, the rock formations at **Casibari** and **Ayó**, huge grey diorite boulders, are another natural tourist attraction.

NATURAL BRIDGE

near Andicouri
On the central north coast, the sea has carved this natural archway, 100 feet (30m) long and 25 feet (8m) high, from the coral rock.

Continue northwest to **Bushiribana**, where the ruins of an old gold mine and smelter can be seen. Gold was mined here in the 19th century, and some historians have speculated that the name Aruba might have been derived from the Spanish *oro uba*, meaning 'there was gold'. However, it is more likely to come from the Amerindian *oruba*, 'well-placed' or · convenient to the mainland.

♦♦♦
THE SOUTHEAST COAST
To the north of San Nicolas, a former oil refinery town, **Commandeur's Bay** is a good dive spot. Near by, the **Guadirikiri** and **Fontein Caves** contain Amerindian hieroglyphs of dubious origin, but they are inevitably included on official round-island tours. The smaller beaches on Aruba's southernmost tip include **Rodger's Beach**, **Baby Beach**, **Batchelor's Beach** and **Boca Grandi** on the Caribbean shore.

Eating Out
Dining out in Aruba is a truly international affair with everything from Chinese to Italian cuisine on offer. To sample real Aruban specialities, head for Palm Beach and **Gasparito**, Gasparito 3 (tel: 297-8/37044), or **Old Cunucu House**, Palm Beach 150 (tel: 297-8/31666), which both serve seafood and local dishes in traditional Aruban houses. Alternatively, elegant **Papiamento**, Washington 61 (tel: 297-8/24544) occupies a lovely 19th-century country house in Noord in the north of the island. Near St Nicolas in the south, sample local home cooking at **Mi Cushina**, Cura Cabai (tel: 297-8/48335; closed Thursday).

BONAIRE
Forty miles (64km) off the coast of Venezuela, Bonaire is the least developed of the ABC Islands, and a mecca for divers. Shaped rather like a boomerang, the island measures 24 miles (38km) from end to end, and a mere 5 miles (8km) at its widest point. Like its sister islands, Bonaire is low-lying and dusty. Its chief charms are of the underwater variety, and most of the coastline is protected as a marine reserve. The best dive sites are found in the sheltered waters off the leeward coast, conveniently close to the tiny island capital of Kralendijk. The main resort areas are also here, leaving the north of the island to the birds and lizards who take refuge in Washington-Slagbaai National Park. Down in the south, the old salt trade, first introduced by colonial settlers, has been revived. Here, the coast road runs past the salt works where sea water is evaporated in shallow salt pans and mounds of salt crystals are bulldozed into huge white dunes to await shipment all over the world.

♦
KRALENDIJK
Set in the protective curve of the boomerang, Kralendijk means 'coral wall', and the port can only be visited by smaller cruise ships. There is shopping on Breedestraat, and a selection of welcoming restaurants and bars spread along the waterfront with views of the uninhabited island of Klein Bonaire and visiting boats from Curaçao. A few traditional gold-painted local-style houses with white stucco

An historical footnote: abandoned slave huts overlooking Pekelmeer Lagoon, Bonaire

trim can be spotted among the newer buildings. Also on the harbourfront, the 19th-century defences of **Fort Oranje** have found peacetime employment as a folklore museum housing Amerindian artefacts and local historical and cultural exhibits. *Instituto Folklorico, Fort Oranje, open:* Monday to Friday 08.00hrs–noon.

BONAIRE MARINE PARK ✓

The main reason most visitors come to Bonaire is for the diving. Reckoned to be one of the top three dive sites in the world, the offshore coral reef landscape is stunning and heavily populated by a wide range of tropical fish and marine creatures. Most hotels provide dive facilities and there are a number of diving centres offering boat trips, equipment

hire, and instruction. Divers pay a nominal fee which helps maintain the underwater park.

◆◆
PEKELMEER
south of Kralendijk
A circular drive leads south along the coast from Kralendijk, past the rosy sands of **Pink Beach**, and on to the salt works centred on the shallow Pekelmeer lagoon. A few 19th-century slave huts have survived near the shore, and one of Bonaire's famous flamingo colonies makes its home down here.

◆◆
WASHINGTON-SLAGBAAI NATIONAL PARK
north of Kralendijk
A former plantation turned natural preserve, the 22-acre (9ha) park is criss-crossed by marked driving and walking trails allowing a close-up look at native fauna. One hike scales Mount Brandaris (785ft/240m), the island's highest point.

Hardy local flora is well-respected in the form of cacti and totrured-looking divi-divi trees sculpted by the wind. Bonaire's notable local birdlife (over 125 species of birds reside on the island) is often rather more difficult to spot, but the **Goto Meer**, just south of the park, is another favourite breeding ground for flamingos.

Eating Out

If you don't want to eat in a hotel, the Kralendijk waterfront is the place to be. The upturned boat hull bar at **Raffles** (tel: 599-7/8617) is a good place to hang out, and seafood is the speciality in the restaurant. Fish and seafood also feature on the menu at **Richard's** (tel: 599-7/5263), but there are local dishes too. Behind the harbour, **Rendez-Vous** (tel: 599-7/8454) has a modern setting, an attractive terrace, and continental or local dishes. The **Kilumba Grill** (tel: 599-7/5019) is a well-priced local spot.

CURAÇAO

The largest of the Netherlands Antilles at 38 miles by 9 miles (61km by 14km), Curaçao has been the chief Dutch island and administrative capital of their Caribbean possessions since the mid-17th century. With little in the way of natural resources, it flourished as both an important trading centre for European and South American merchants and a leading Caribbean slave market until abolition. As in Aruba, the 20th-century oil boom revived the island's fortunes, but now Curaçao depends on tourism offering diving from sites along the leeward coast and several low-key attractions, such as restored *landhuisen* (country houses) and the Curaçao Liqueur Distillery, which produces the famous liqueur found behind cocktail bars the world over.

Elegant colonial architecture on display in Willemstad

◆◆◆
WILLEMSTAD

Willemstad's waterfront, the **Handelskade**, looks like an elaborate slice of Amsterdam sculpted from ice cream. Dutch gabled houses painted in shades of strawberry, pistachio and vanilla-yellow line the quay. It is said a 19th-century governor ordained the pastel colour scheme as sunshine reflecting off brilliant whitewash hurt his eyes.

The Otrobanda district, where cruise ships dock, is linked to the Handelskade by the 555-foot (170m) **Koningin Emmabrug**, one of the world's largest movable pontoon bridges when the original was installed in 1888. Behind Handelskade, the **Punda** is the oldest part of town and main shopping district, and to the north there is a daily floating market where Venezuelan schooners offload fresh produce.

To the south, **Fort Amsterdam** dates from the late 17th century. Visitors are welcome to take a look around the courtyard and fort church. The **Mikveh Israel-Emmanuel Synagogue**, on Columbusstraat, is the oldest synagogue in the Americas. It was founded in 1732 and has a small Jewish historical museum. In the 18th-century Otrobanda district, the **Curaçao Museum**, Van Leeuwenhoekstraat, exhibits Amerindian artefacts, colonial furniture, maps, paintings and Delft china in a restored seamen's hospital. *Curaçao Museum open*: Tuesday to Saturday 09.00hrs–noon and 14.00–17.00hrs; Sunday 10.00–16.00hrs.

Jewish Historical Museum open: Monday to Friday 09.00–11.45hrs and 14.30–17.00hrs.

◆◆
CHRISTOFFEL NATIONAL PARK
northwest of Willemstad

A 4,500-acre (1,825ha) tract of dry and dusty *cunucu* backcountry encompassing three former plantation estates, the park would make a dramatic set for a Western movie. At its heart, the Christoffelberg (1,220ft/372m) is the highest point on the island, and there are driving and walking trails through the scrub and cacti. By the old Landhuis Savonet, near the entrance to the park, a museum houses Amerindian exhibits and provides an introduction to local fauna and flora including rare native deer (*bina*), iguanas, lizards and many of Curaçao's 500 or so different plant and flower species. There are regular ranger-led walking and wildlife tours (reservations and schedules, tel: 599-9/640363). *Open*: Monday to Saturday 08.00–17.00hrs; Sunday 06.00–15.00hrs.

◆
CURAÇAO LIQUEUR DISTILLERY
Landhuis Chobolobo (east of Willemstad)

The distillery is a modest operation housed in a fine old 17th-century *landhuis* (country house) on the outskirts of the capital. After a look around the vats and bottling plant, there are tastings and sales. The original (and best-selling) sticky liqueur

is flavoured with small green oranges.
Open: Monday to Friday 08.00hrs–noon and 13.00–16.45hrs.

CURAÇAO SEAQUARIUM
Bapor Kibra (south of Willemstad)
A chance to meet local marine life face to face without getting wet. Tanks contain over 400 varieties of tropical fish, crabs, sponges and corals, and there is a turtle pool.
The protected waters of the neighbouring **Curaçao Underwater Park** afford excellent diving opportunities. There are glass-bottomed boat trips, too, and a good swimming beach.
Open: daily, 10.00–22.00hrs.

◆◆◆

LANDHUIS BRIEVENGAT
northeast of Willemstad
Over 80 old Dutch Colonial-style country houses (*landhuisen*) lie dotted around Curaçao. The 18th-century Landhuis Brievengat, on a former cochineal plantation, is one of the best. It has been carefully restored and is open for tours and Friday evening dinner dances. On the last Sunday of the month, there is a folkloric show at 17.00hrs (tel: 599-9/378344).
Open: daily, 09.15–12.15hrs and 15.00–18.00hrs.

Eating Out
Literally top of the pile in a wonderful position above Willemstad, **Fort Nassau** (tel: 599-9/613450) is one of

Curaçao's finest gourmet dining rooms; and the **Bistro Le Clochard**, Riffort (tel: 599-9/625666) serves excellent French cuisine in 18th-century fortress dungeons. Rather less pricey, **Fort Waakzaamheid**, Berg Domi (tel: 599-9/623633) offers grilled food with great views. **Chez Suzanne**, Blomonteweg 1 (tel: 599-9/688545), and **Golden Star**, Socratesstraat 2 (tel: 599-9/654795) are both recommended for local dishes such as *balchi piska* (fishballs). Locals themselves often pop into the **Cactus Club**, Van Staverenweg 6 (tel: 599-9/371600) for burgers and cocktails; and also **Rum Runners**, De Rouvilleweg 9F (tel: 599-9/623038), a lively bar and restaurant on the Otrobanda waterfront.

Marine Life
The Caribbean region offers a handful of the best dive sites in the world. Around 75 different species of corals form spectacular reefs where branches of staghorn coral, rippling sea whips, sponges and the uncannily lifelike brain coral play host to darting shoals of exotically painted tropical fish, turtles, lobsters and sinister-looking eels tucked into dark crevices. The best diving and snorkelling in the region can be found off Bonaire, Curaçao, Saba, the Virgin Islands, the Bahama Islands, and, perhaps best of all, the Cayman Islands, where the famous Cayman Wall drops 20,000 feet (6,000m) down to the bottom of the ocean.

SABA

A rugged volcanic peak rising almost sheer from the sea 30 miles (50km) south of Sint Maarten, Saba is the smallest of the Netherlands Antilles measuring a mere 5 square miles (13sq km). Saba is quiet and rural, dominated by the towering green bulk of Mount Scenery (2,885ft/880m), with four small villages of whitewashed and red-roofed houses clinging to the foothills. The island has no beaches, luxury resorts or international shopping emporiums, but its fans rave about the diving and blissfully relaxed pace of life. First settled by the Dutch in 1640, Saba changed hands several times before being secured permanently by the Netherlands in 1816. However, the island's dramatic topography and inhospitable coastline meant the changes occurred on paper rather than as the result of force and Saba remains something of an impregnable fortress with two man-made harbours and a tiny landing strip that is not recommended for the faint-hearted. The island's tortuous switchback roads are minor miracles of engineering built by the locals after Dutch road builders from the mainland just threw up their hands in horror and claimed the task to be impossible. It is not difficult to appreciate their point of view.

Eye-catching decorative detail on a traditional Saban cottage

THE BOTTOM

Over 500 steps scale the cliffs from Ladder Bay up to The Bottom, Saba's minuscule capital; and there is a similarly taxing perpendicular ascent from the island's main port at Fort Bay. The Bottom actually takes its name from the volcanic hollow it sits in, surrounded by forested peaks and hills. The island's administrative offices are here, along with the Lieutenant Governor's attractive West Indian residence with gingerbread ornamentation. Other timber-frame buildings house a small selection of shops and local bars.

MOUNT SCENERY

west of Windwardside
The Stairwell, a 1,064-step trail, ascends Mount Scenery cutting through exuberant rainforest vegetation thick with huge golden heliconias, ferns, mango and banana trees, also orchids in winter. Near the top, in stunted elfin forest, twisted tree trunks support dozens of mosses and bromeliads. The best time to climb Mount Scenery is a clear day, when the views are spectacular.

SABA MARINE PARK

access from Fort Bay
Established in 1987, the marine park encircles the entire island and offers spectacular reef diving with pristine conditions and excellent visibility. There are 29 permanent mooring buoys for the dive boats which depart from Fort Bay.

WINDWARDSIDE

east of The Bottom
From The Bottom, Saba's rollercoaster cross-island land route, simply known as The Road, rises, falls and wriggles its way to the island's second village nestled 2,000 feet (600m) up in the mountains. The tourist office and several hotels are located here among winding streets where cottage gardens, brilliant with hibiscus flowers and bougainvillaea, threaten to burst their stone walls. One century-old house has been turned into the **Saba Museum**, which juxtaposes Amerindian artefacts with colonial furnishings and an antique organ. The village craft shops are a good place to buy Saban handmade lace, which is actually intricate embroidery used to decorate linen.
Museum open: Monday to Friday 10.00hrs–noon and 13.00–15.30hrs.

Eating Out

Saba's charming inns all have good dining rooms (reservations recommended). The nicest place to dine in The Bottom is **Cranston's Antique Inn** (tel: 599-4/63203), in an old West Indian house; while **Queenie's Serving Spoon** (tel: 599-4/63225) dishes up no-nonsense local food. In Windwardside, **Captain's Quarters** (tel: 599-4/62201) offers good food and terrace dining in an old sea captain's house. **Scout's Place** (tel: 599-4/62205) is relaxed and friendly; and the **Brigadoon Restaurant** (tel: 599-4/62380) specialises in local and Creole dishes.

SINT EUSTATIUS

Tiny Statia (pronounced *Stay-sha*), as the island is more commonly known, was once a Caribbean honeypot. During the 18th century, it was nicknamed the Golden Rock, and dozens of merchant ships rode at anchor in the bay, while the mile-long (1.6km) string of warehouses along the shore below Oranjestad was packed from floor to ceiling with silver, guns, sugar and silks.

On 16 November 1776, the American brig *Andrew Doria* sailed into Oranjestad Bay and loosed off a 13-gun salute marking American independence from Britain. Statia's governor, Johannes de Graaff, responded, making the island the first country in the world to recognise the United States, and earning Statia the soubriquet 'America's Childhood Friend'. However, the gesture ultimately brought about the island's downfall when Britain retaliated in the shape of Admiral Rodney, who attacked the island in 1781, pillaged the warehouses, and destroyed Statia's fortunes for good.

Today, Statia is a sleepy backwater, 30 miles (48km) south of Sint Maarten. There is little development, only a handful of hotels, and the island's few beaches are dark and volcanic. Favourite diversions include diving and walking, particularly in the south part of the island where the extinct volcanic cone of Mount Mazinga, or The Quill, offers several easy walking trails.

ORANJESTAD

Oranjestad's Lower Town, where several old waterfront warehouses are undergoing restoration, is divided from the Upper Town by a 100-foot (30m) cliff. On the upper level, traditional wooden buildings, the ruins of the stone-built Honen Dalim Synagogue and the belltower of the Dutch Reformed Church gather in the lee of the old fort. **Fort Oranje** was founded by the Dutch in 1636, and has been in danger of falling down the cliff ever since. However, it still houses the island's administrative offices and affords splendid views.

Admiral Rodney made his headquarters in the historic Jan Simonsz Donckerhuis, on Van Tonningenweg, now home to the **St Eustatius Historical Foundation Museum**. Artefacts on display range from Arawak finds to colonial furniture and the

The Old Gin House Hotel in Statia's capital, Oranjestad

little blue beads which once served as currency in the slave market.

Museum open: Monday to Friday 09.00–17.00hrs; Saturday and Sunday 09.00hrs–noon.

◆◆◆
THE QUILL

walking access from Welfare Road, south of Oranjestad
The best of Statia's dozen or so walking trails is a 45-minute hike up to The Quill's crater rim, 2,000 feet (600m) above sea level. It can get quite slippery along the way, but inside the crater bowl there is a luxuriant rainforest jungle of giant mahogany and breadfruit trees wreathed with lianas and spreading carpets of mosses and ferns. The locals come here at night to hunt land-crabs, a Statian culinary treat.

Eating Out

Down in the Lower Town, **The Old Gin House** (tel: 599-3/82319) occupies a restored 18th-century warehouse and offers an excellent Continental menu in attractive, antique-furnished surroundings. The **King's Well Restaurant**, Bay Road (tel: 599-3/82538) has a breezy veranda and offers US and Austrian specialities; or, in the Upper Town, **L'Etoile**, Heiligerweg (tel: 599-3/82299), and the **Stone Oven Bar and Restaurant**, Faeschweg (tel: 599-3/82543) serve island cuisine. Across the island on the east coast, **La Maison sur la Plage**, Zeelandia Beach (tel: 599-3/82256) combines lovely views from the airy, trellised restaurant with French food.

SINT MAARTEN/SAINT-MARTIN

A recipe for schizophrenia, Sint Maarten/Saint-Martin is the smallest island in the world (37sq miles/96sq km) to be divided between two sovereign states. The Dutch–French division dates back to 1648, and although France got the lion's share (21sq miles/54sq km), relations are amicable and the island is one of the most prosperous and developed enclaves in the Caribbean. There are no border controls between the two halves of the island, but French Saint-Martin maintains a particularly Gallic flavour (and topless beaches), while Sint Maarten is more international. Dutch, French and English are all widely spoken.

◆◆◆
SINT MAARTEN ✓

The Dutch capital, **Philipsburg**, is the main entry point to the island, a top cruise ship destination and second only to St Thomas (USVI) in the lucrative duty-free shopping stakes. The main action takes place on Front Street, an appealing mile-long (1.6km) shopper's paradise.
The **Sint Maarten Museum**, 119 Front Street, is laid out in a century-old wooden house. Exhibits trace island history from Amerindian times.
Sint Maarten's best beaches stretch out along the coast northwest of town. The road heads out past **Cole Bay** and **Simpson Bay** to the tourist favourite **Mullet Bay**, with a wide range of watersports, shops and a golf course.

◆◆
SAINT-MARTIN

Only the West Indian stallholders and their wares laid out in waterfront market give any hint that **Marigot** is a Caribbean town not a sunny corner of mainland France. The attractive, small and relaxed (in comparison with teeming Philipsburg) capital of Saint-Martin boasts sidewalk cafés and shops overlooking the water, and the ruins of 18th-century **Fort St-Louis**. Deep-sea fishing trips and day cruises depart from the **Port La Royale Marina**, to the west of town. Saint-Martin's coastline offers a choice of excellent beaches. **Baie Nettlé**, **Baie Rouge**, and the stunning sand strip of **Baie Longue** lie to the west. Northeast of Marigot, the town of **Grand-Case** is renowned for its restaurants, and then the road circles around the north of the island and landmark **Pic du Paradis** to the Atlantic Coast beaches of **Baie de l'Orient** (nudists), **Baie de l'Embouchure** (windsurfing and snorkelling), and **Baie Lucas** (snorkelling).

Free as a bird: windsurfing off the coast of Sint Maarten

Eating Out

Philipsburg's Front Street is Sint Maarten's restaurant row. Two top dining spots here are **Antoine's** (tel: 599-5/22964) for fine French cuisine; and **Da Livio** (tel: 599-5/22960), which serves an Italian menu on the waterfront. For a taste of the Dutch East Indies, sample Indonesian fare at **Wajang Doll** (tel: 599-5/22687). In Saint-Martin, Marigot has the excellent **Poisson d'Or** (tel: 590/87 72 45) in a restored waterfront warehouse; and **Maison sur le Port** (tel: 590/87 56 38) with a pretty terrace. In Grand-Case, **Le Tastevin** (tel: 590/87 55 45) is a gourmet haunt and there is good seafood at **Fish Pot** (tel: 590/87 50 88). NB When telephoning from the Dutch side to the French side, dial 06 followed by the six-figure local number; when calling from the French side to the Dutch, dial 3 followed by the number.

THE BAHAMA ISLANDS

The 700 Bahama Islands (and several thousand more rocky islets and cays) appear 50 miles (80km) off the coast of Florida and stretch southeast for over 750 miles (1,200km). Only around 20 of the islands are inhabited, with most of the population of 255,000 crowded onto the islands of Grand Bahama and New Providence, where the cruise ship ports of Freeport and Nassau are among the busiest in the region. Christopher Columbus first set foot in the New World in the Bahamas, on 12 October 1492, and the archipelago is named after the Spanish for 'shallow sea' (*baja mar*). British Puritans founded the first settlement on Eleuthera in 1648, before moving to New Providence, and the islands were a veritable pirates' lair in the 17th and 18th centuries, later providing a safe haven for Loyalists after the American War of Independence, Civil War gunrunners and Prohibition rumrunners. The Bahamas achieved independence from Britain in 1973. Though they remain part of the Commonwealth, the US influence is strong. Tourism and offshore finance are the islands' chief revenue sources.

GRAND BAHAMA
The fourth-largest of the Bahama Islands, measuring 96 miles (154km) from end to end, Grand Bahama made the leap from fishermen's backwater to international resort in a couple of decades under the stewardship of American entrepreneur Wallace Groves. The south coast

Bahamanian signpost tree

of the island is fringed by miles of pristine beaches, and there is excellent diving and fishing. Duty-free shopping is another major attraction for the many cruise ship passengers who flock ashore here.

FREEPORT/LUCAYA
Grand Bahama's main city, Freeport, and its beach resort annexe, Lucaya, are built along the American model. The broad boulevards are lined with highrise hotels and shopping malls, there are international restaurants aplenty, and local nightlife features cabarets and casinos. The top attraction in town is the **International Bazaar**, a 10-acre (4ha) open-air shopping complex featuring eclectic architecture, stores piled high

with luxury goods selling at around 20–40 per cent below US retail prices, and local souvenirs in the Straw Market. **Port Lucaya** is another top shopping, dining and entertainment stop with a busy marina and regular glass-bottomed boat trips out to the coral reefs.

For an escape from the mercantile mayhem, take a stroll around the 100-acre (40ha) **Rand Memorial Nature Centre**, home to 21 species of wild orchids and rich birdlife including flamingos.
Nature Centre open: Monday to Friday 09.00–16.00hrs; guided tours 10.00hrs and 14.00hrs.

◆◆
GARDEN OF THE GROVES AND GRAND BAHAMA MUSEUM
Midshipman Road, east of Freeport
Twelve landscaped acres (5ha) of exotic flowers and shrubs, palm trees and pools fed by miniature waterfalls. Within the garden, the **Grand Bahama Museum** covers local history and culture through displays of Lucayan Indian artefacts left by the island's original inhabitants, sections on pirates and marine life, and elaborate Junkanoo costumes worn in the annual carnival (see box, page 73).
Open: daily, 09.00–16.00hrs.

◆
LUCAYAN NATIONAL PARK
near Gold Rock, east of Freeport
The world's largest explored underwater cave system lies beneath this central island park. The main attraction is a pair of limestone sink-holes and there are trails through areas of scrub vegetation, forest and mangroves.
Open: daily.

Taking time out at Freeport's International Bazaar

◆◆◆
UNEXSO (UNDERWATER EXPLORERS SOCIETY)
Port Lucaya
Top island dive operators, UNEXSO, run a dive school; dive trips to reefs, wrecks and night dives; a Museum of Diving History; and boat trips to **The Dolphin Experience**. It is a 20-minute ride to the dolphin facility at Sanctuary Bay, where Atlantic bottlenose dolphins can be observed close to and petted. There are dolphin dives, too. For schedules (reservations advised), tel: 242/373 1240.

Breathtaking underwater scenery on the Caribbean reefs

Eating Out
In Freeport itself, the International Bazaar offers a wide choice of dining with a suitably international flavour, from the **Japanese Steak House** (tel: 242/352 9521) to **Café Michael** (tel: 242/352 2191) for French and Bahamanian dishes. **Ruby Swiss**, W Sunrise Highway and Atlantic Way (tel: 242/352 8507) is a Bahamanian gourmet haunt; while **The Captain's Charthouse Restaurant and Lounge**,

E Sunrise Highway and Beachway Drive (tel: 242/373 3900) serves up Bahamanian lobster, steaks, and a dinner show. Around Lucaya there is plenty of hotel dining, such as the Port Lucaya Resort and Yacht Club, Bell Channel Bay Road, where the **Tradewinds Café** (tel: 242/373 6618) specialises in Caribbean and Floridian cuisine. Check out the lively **Junkanoo Bar and Grill**, Port Lucaya Marketplace (tel: 242/373 6170); or try local specialities at **Banana Bay**, Fortune Beach (tel: 242/373 2960). **The Stoned Crab**, Taino Beach (tel: 242/373 1442) is an excellent bet for fresh seafood with ocean views.

Junkanoo

Every Caribbean island celebrates Carnival at some point in the year – usually in the run-up to Lent – but in the Bahama Islands it is known as Junkanoo and runs from Boxing Day through to the New Year. Born out of ancient African traditions, Junkanoo is a great opportunity to dress up in elaborate costumes and party. There are 'rush' parades through the streets of Freeport and Nassau on 26 December, and again on New Year's Day. Decorated floats, dancers and bands are urged on by Goombay rhythms, drums and piercing whistles. All sorts of beauty pageants and competitions take place in the intervening days.
On the Nassau waterfront, Junkanoo Expo, Prince George Dock, exhibits a year-round display of Junkanoo costumes, arts and crafts.

NEW PROVIDENCE

When the Puritan settlement on Eleuthera failed, its leader, William Sayle, relocated to a fine natural harbour on the north coast of New Providence, which became Nassau, the capital of the Bahamas. A fraction of the size of Grand Bahama at 21 miles by 7 miles (33km by 11km), New Providence has far more to offer on the sightseeing front, and a colonial background more similar to its Caribbean neighbours.

◆◆◆
NASSAU ✓

Cruise ships literally queue up to spill their human cargo onto the Nassau dockside. It is a short walk to **Rawson Square**, where horse-drawn carriages wait in the shade to whisk visitors off on a guided tour of the historic town. Just across Bay Street, Bahamanian administrators meet in the pink-and-white colonial-style House of Assembly, the Supreme Court and the Ministry of Finance, grouped around **Parliament Square**. Bustling Bay Street runs parallel to the waterfront offering wall-to-wall shopping and the touristy but ever-popular **Straw Market**, a bountiful source of hand-woven island souvenirs and T-shirts. It is easy to explore Nassau's colonial monuments on foot. At the western end of Bay Street, look for 18th-century **Vendue House**, the former slave auction house which now exhibits paintings by local folk artist Amos Ferguson, and historical

displays in the Pompey Museum. There is more on local history at the **Bahamas Historical Society**, Shirley Street and Elizabeth Avenue. From Bay Street, George Street leads up past the Anglican **Christ Church Cathedral** to the Governor-General's 'Nassau pink' residence, **Government House**. To the southeast, **Fort Fincastle** looks like a little stone ship run aground on the hillside. Built in 1793, it was never called upon to fire a shot in anger, but made a convenient lighthouse and lookout. For a broader panoramic view, take the elevator up to the observation deck of the adjacent Water Tower, the highest point on the island (216ft/66m). Then descend the 66-step **Queen's Staircase**, hewn out of the limestone by 18th-century slaves.
Bahamas Historical Society open: Monday to Wednesday and Friday 10.00–16.00hrs; Saturday 10.00hrs–noon.
Fort Fincastle and Water Tower open: daily, dawn to dusk.
Vendue House open: Monday to Friday 10.00–16.30hrs; Saturday 10.00–13.00hrs.

◆

ARDASTRA GARDENS AND ZOO
Chippingham Road, west of downtown Nassau
Five acres (2ha) of tropical gardens and a zoo full of monkeys, snakes, iguanas and birds, including the native Bahama parrot. This is also the place to catch the famous 'Marching Flamingos' (the

Bahamas' national bird) being put through their drill at thrice-daily Flamingo Shows (11.00, 14.00 and 16.00hrs).
Open: daily, 09.00–17.00hrs.

◆◆◆
CABLE BEACH
3 miles (5km) west of Nassau
The island's resort headquarters (frequent buses from Bay Street in Nassau) is a magnificent sweep of sand lined by huge and luxurious hotels. Every tourist whim is catered for here from watersports and glass-bottomed boat trips to dining and dancing the night away.

◆◆◆
CORAL WORLD
Silver Cay, west of Nassau
An amazing introduction to the underwater world with two dozen aquariums, shark tanks, stingray and turtle pools, a huge artificial reef tank and an underwater observatory sunk 20 feet (6m) below sea level. Snorkellers can paddle out along the Pleasure Reef Snorkelling Trail (there is equipment rental, changing rooms and lessons for beginners).
Open: daily, 09.00–18.00hrs.

◆◆
FORT CHARLOTTE
1 mile (1.6km) west of Nassau, off West Bay Street
Dating from 1788, the fort's low whitewashed walls spread along the crest of the bluff surrounded by a dry moat. Like Fort Fincastle, Fort Charlotte never saw action, but the battlements are manned by an impressive battery of cannon, and the stone

walls, including the dungeons, are scarred with antique grafitti chiselled away by bored 19th-century soldiers.
Open: Monday to Saturday 09.00–16.00hrs.

PARADISE ISLAND
toll causeway or ferries from Nassau
Across Nassau Harbour, the former Hog Island underwent a cosmetic name change in the 1960s when the hotel developers stepped in. There are good beaches and watersports galore, a golf club and horse-riding opportunities. Near the eastern end of Paradise Island Drive, the **Versailles Gardens** are landscaped with terraces, pools, fountains and statuary. The showpiece is the French Cloisters, hijacked from a 14th-century monastery in the French pilgrim town of Lourdes, shipped across the Atlantic and rebuilt stone by stone.

Eating Out
Right in the heart of downtown Nassau, **Pick-A-Dilly**, Parliament Street (tel: 242/322 2836) is a longtime favourite for island food and serious daiquiris; or opt for informal waterfront dining at **Le Shack**, Day Street (tel: 242/325 2148). **Buena Vista**, Delancey Street (tel: 242/322 2811) and **Graycliff**, West Hill Street (tel: 242/322 2796) are two of the best restaurants on the island, both set in fine old colonial houses.
On Paradise Island, the swish Atlantis resort (tel: 242/363 2518) has a dozen restaurants, including **Café Martinique** for

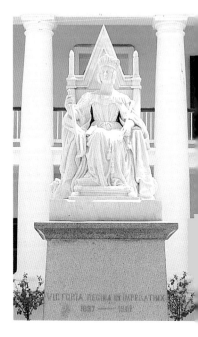

Queen Victoria's Statue on Parliament Square, Nassau

French gourmet cuisine, and the buffet at **Seagrapes**. The Ocean Club's **Courtyard Terrace**, Paradise Island Drive (tel: 242/363 2518) has a waterfront setting; and there is **Columbus Tavern** at the Paradise Harbour Club and Marina, Paradise Island Drive (tel: 242/363 2534). The Cable Beach hotels are also good dining options; or there is the lively restaurant-bar at **Dicky Mo's Deck**, West Bay Street (tel: 242/327 7854); and for daytime dining with ocean views, Coral World's waterfront **Clipper Restaurant**, Silver Cay (tel: 242/328 1036) serves salads, burgers and seafood.

OTHER CRUISING ISLANDS

BARBADOS

One hundred miles (160km) east of the Windward Island chain, Barbados was ruled by the British for three uninterrupted centuries, and the colonial legacy of cane fields and plantation houses, incongruously familiar place names and the game of cricket lives on alongside the Bajans' distinctly relaxed and friendly lifestyle. Despite being completely surrounded by the Atlantic Ocean, the pear-shaped island, measuring 21 miles by 14 miles (33km by 22km), has a definite windward and leeward side. The leeward west coast is home to the best beaches and smartest resorts; the south coast is renowned for its lively atmosphere and nightlife; and the rocky, wave-lashed east coast is the least developed, with picturesque headlands and coves. Inland Barbados is quiet and rural, with pockets of mahogany forest and open grazing land rising to the hilly Scotland district in the northeast.

◆

BRIDGETOWN

The energetic island capital, home to around half the 250,000-strong population, focuses on the The Careenage, a natural inner harbour where the first British settlers found an Amerindian bridge in 1625. On the northern waterfront, at the top of the Broad Street shopping district, Trafalgar Square is overlooked by a statue of Lord Nelson, and the Parliament Buildings which date from the 1870s. Near by, St Michael's Cathedral, built between 1784 and 1786, records snippets of island history in its numerous inscribed tombstones and tablets. A mile (1.6km) south of the city centre, the **Garrison Savannah** district makes an interesting visit. The former British army parade ground has been turned into a race course, its grassy track surrounded by imposing 19th-century buildings and the ruins of two old forts. The entertaining **Barbados Museum**

Onlookers take a keen interest in a roadside game of dominoes

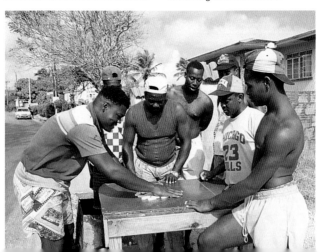

Lord Nelson surveys Bridgetown from Trafalgar Square

is housed in the old military prison, an elegant Caribbean Georgian building flanked by palms. Historical exhibits include a fascinating collection of West Indian prints and paintings dating back to the 1600s.
Barbados Museum open: Monday to Saturday 10.00–18.00hrs; Sunday 14.00–18.00hrs.

◆◆◆
ANDROMEDA GARDENS
east coast, near Bathsheba, St Joseph District
These most glorious botanical gardens, founded in 1954, represent one of the finest collections of indigenous and exotic tropical trees and plants in the Caribbean. Winding paths criss-cross the steep hillside site, with glimpses of the ocean below, climbing through orchid gardens and heliconia and hibiscus areas to shady corners irrigated by tiny streams and waterfalls.
Open: daily, 09.00–17.00hrs.

◆
ANIMAL FLOWER CAVE
north coast, St Lucy District
Dozens of tiny multicoloured sea anemones 'flower' in the pools of this underground cavern hollowed out of the cliffs. Visitors can scramble about the rocks, and take a dip in the swimming hole.
Open: daily, 09.00–17.00hrs.

◆◆
BARBADOS WILDLIFE RESERVE, GRENADE HALL SIGNAL STATION AND FOREST
Farley Hill, St Peter District
Vervet monkeys, brocket deer, otters, porcupines and iguanas are among the many and varied inhabitants of the 4-acre (1.6ha) mahogany forest reserve, and they are free to wander wherever they choose. For safety's sake the python remains behind bars, and the alligator-like caimans are confined to their pool, but otherwise there is real wildlife spotting to be done exploring the woodlands. Across the car park, the old Signal Station was one of six lookout towers erected in the early 1800s to relay messages from one side of the island to the other using semaphore flags. Nature trails meander through the adjacent Grenade Hall Forest.
Open: daily, 10.00–17.00hrs.

◆
CODRINGTON COLLEGE
east coast, St John District
A former Governor of the Leeward Islands, Christopher Codrington, endowed the 18th-century theological college which now spreads out around

OTHER CRUISING ISLANDS

There are fine views from the Morgan Lewis Sugar Mill

his 17th-century childhood home. The approach, down an avenue of tall and slender palms, is magnificent and the grounds, with waterlily ponds and a forest trail, are open to the public.
Open: daily, 10.00–16.00hrs.

FARLEY HILL PARK
St Peter District
Surrounding the ruins of a grand plantation mansion built for the visit of Prince Albert in 1861, the park is a favourite picnic spot with terrific views.
Open: daily, 08.30–18.00hrs.

◆◆
FRANCIA PLANTATION HOUSE AND GUN HILL SIGNAL STATION
St George District
A turn-of-the-century great house, Francia still lords it over a working plantation, while its lovely terraced gardens overlook the St George valley. Guided tours of the house take in a notable collection of antique prints and one of the earliest maps of the Caribbean region, dating from 1522.
Near by, the **Gun Hill Signal Station** houses a collection of military memorabilia. On the road below, the stone lion statue was carved by Captain Henry Wilkinson in 1868.
Francia open: Monday to Friday 10.00–16.00hrs.
Gun Hill open: Monday to Saturday 09.00–17.00hrs.

◆◆
HARRISON'S CAVE
St Joseph District
A series of dramatic limestone caverns in the centre of the island, this is a good place to cool off and goggle at the bizarre and theatrically illuminated rock formations. A tram makes the rounds of the subterranean kingdom winding down to a pool fed by a 40-foot (12m) waterfall.
Open: daily, 09.00–16.00hrs.

◆
MORGAN LEWIS SUGAR MILL
St Peter District
The largest surviving windmill in the Caribbean region, the Morgan Lewis mill was one of the island's 300 sugar-grinding mills in the 17th century. A working mill right up until 1944, the machinery has been restored, and there are grand views across the rolling countryside from the sail loft.
Open: Monday to Friday 09.00–17.00hrs.

◆◆◆
ST NICHOLAS ABBEY
St Peter District
A mid-17th-century great house with no religious conotations but a wonderful Jacobean gabled façade, the Abbey is the oldest historic home on the island. Guided tours of the antique-filled ground floor reveal all sorts of fascinating period detail; try to catch the short home movie depicting Bridgetown and plantation life in 1935 (11.30 and 14.30hrs).
Open: Monday to Friday 10.00–15.00hrs.

◆◆
WELCHMAN HALL GULLY
St Thomas District
A mile-long (1.6km) botanical walk in a lush, densely wooded gully in the centre of the island, Welchman Hall was originally laid out in the 1860s. Native plant species have been augmented with bamboos, spice plants and exotic ferns, and although a few flowering plants have been added, the main effect is cool and green.
Open: daily, 09.00–17.00hrs.

Eating Out
Barbados' swish west coast hotels all have good restaurants, but one of the loveliest settings on the island is elegant **Bagatelle Great House**, St James (tel: 246/421 6767); and for gourmet dining on the waterfront, **Carambola**, St James (tel: 246/432 0832). In Bridgetown, the **Waterfront Café**, The Careenage (tel: 246/427 0093) offers a broad menu of Bajan and Creole dishes, pasta and salads. Down on the south coast, overlooking St Lawrence Bay, **David's Place**, Christ Church (tel: 246/435 9755) serves fine Bajan cuisine; **Pisces**, St Lawrence Gap (tel: 246/435 6564) is renowned for seafood and local dishes; and there is always a lively scene and local bands nightly at **The Ship Inn Pub**, St Lawrence Gap (tel: 246/435 6961).

Rum
That ubiquitous Caribbean spirit distilled from molasses, the treacly substance left after the sugar has been extracted from cane juice, has been made in Barbados since the 1640s. Though rum is produced throughout the islands, the full-flavoured dark rums of Barbados and Jamaica are considered the best. In the French islands, fine rums are laid down and matured like brandy. A popular stop on any Barbadian sightseeing itinerary is a tour followed by tastings at the Mount Gay Rum Visitors' Centre, Spring Garden Highway, Bridgetown (*open*: Monday to Friday 09.00–16.00hrs).

OTHER CRUISING ISLANDS

BERMUDA

Cast adrift in the Atlantic Ocean, 1,000 miles (1,600km) northeast of the Caribbean, the Bermuda Islands stretch in a 22-mile (35km) curve of islets and coral cays warmed by the Gulf Stream. Bermuda itself has three cruise ship docks: Hamilton; the Royal Naval Dockyard; and St George. During the busy summer season (April to November), many ships stop in at two of the ports during a week-long visit.

A British colony for four centuries, Bermuda was discovered in 1503, but not settled until the early 17th century after Sir George Somers was shipwrecked *en route* to America. Subsequently, the British introduced Georgian architecture, pubs, cricket and Bermuda shorts (a 19th-century military innovation). The Bermudians are renowned for their friendliness, and the islands offer numerous sightseeing opportunities, pink coral sand beaches, excellent diving, and the greatest concentration of golf courses in the world.

◆◆
HAMILTON

Bermuda's capital and chief cruise port is the communications hub of the island with bus and ferry links to all points of interest (there are no hire cars on Bermuda). The first stop for many visitors is Front Street, a colourful parade of shops housed in pastel-painted colonial buildings sporting flagpoles topped by the Union Flag. Horse-drawn carriage tours depart from here, and look for the famous Birdcage, at the

junction with Queen Street, where a Bermuda shorts-clad policeman directs the traffic. On Church Street, the tower of **Bermuda Cathedral** affords a panoramic view of the town and sheltered waters of Great Sound.

A short walk away, the collections of the **Bermuda National Gallery** are on display in City Hall. There are works by Gainsborough and Reynolds, as well as paintings of Bermuda by Winslow Homer and Georgia O'Keefe.

Flying the flag at the Royal Bermuda Yacht Club

Bermuda National Gallery open: Monday to Saturday 10.00–16.00hrs; Sunday 12.30–16.00hrs.

OTHER CRUISING ISLANDS

◆◆
BERMUDA AQUARIUM, MUSEUM AND ZOO

Flatts Village, Harrington Sound
A chance to meet exotic reef fish, tiny seahorses, moray eels and barracuda face to face through the glass. Pet a giant turtle in the zoo; be deafened by the raucous, free-ranging peacocks; and learn about Bermuda's old-time whaling industry and underwater exploration in the museum.
Open: daily, 09.00–17.00hrs.

◆◆
BERMUDA BOTANICAL GARDENS

Paget (east of Hamilton)
Thirty-six colourful acres (14.5ha) of tropical plants and trees, over 1,000 varieties in all, many of which were first introduced by 18th- and 19th-century seafarers. Other attractions include an aviary, an

Great escape: one of Bermuda's many secluded coves

aromatic garden for the blind, and the Premier's official residence, **Camden**, built in 1755.
Open: Tuesday, Wednesday and Friday (closed Wednesday November to March) 09.00–17.00hrs; Camden, Tuesday and Friday noon–14.30hrs.

◆
CRYSTAL CAVES

off Harrington Sound Road, near Church Bay
A cool and eerie world of dripping stalactites and giant stalagmites awaits visitors to these limestone caverns. Walkways traverse deep saltwater pools which reflect the hanging forest of needle-like rock formations above.
Open: daily, 09.30–16.30hrs.

FORT ST CATHERINE MUSEUM

Barry Road, St George's Island

At the northern tip of Bermuda, Fort St Catherine rises sheer from the rocky shore. The fort was founded in 1614, and continually fortified in line with current military thinking through to a major reconstruction in 1865. Today, the massive 25-foot- (7.5m) thick walls contain an historical museum with a military bias, and replicas of the British Crown Jewels.

Open: daily, 10.00–16.00hrs.

Fort St Catherine guards the northern approach to Bermuda

ROYAL NAVAL DOCKYARD AND BERMUDA MARITIME MUSEUM

West End

Developed as part of the Duke of Wellington's grand scheme to fortify Bermuda as the 'Gibraltar of the West', work on the Georgian dockyard began in 1809. Today, the meticulously restored ordnance buildings and barracks have taken on a new lease of life as a sightseeing, shopping, dining and entertainment complex. The island's seafaring history comes under the microscope at the excellent **Bermuda Maritime Museum** laid out in a 19th-century powder magazine.

Exhibits run the gamut from intricate model ships and whaling memorabilia to tales of piracy on the high seas and the Tucker Treasure salvaged from a 16th-century Spanish wreck. *Maritime Museum open*: daily, 10.00–16.30hrs (from 09.30hrs May to November).

◆◆◆ ST GEORGE ✓

St George's Island
The first capital of Bermuda (it transferred to Hamilton in 1815), St George was the second English town to be established in the New World after Jamestown, Virginia. Pretty as a picture, it clusters around the waterfront, facing Ordnance Island and a full-size replica of Sir George Somers' ship *Deliverance* (open to visitors). The shipwrecked Somers and his crew built the original vessel out of salvaged timber during 1609–10, and continued their voyage to America, before returning to colonise the island. Kings Square is the heart of town, presided over by the 1782 Town Hall with its brace of outdoor staircases. The oldest existing building in Bermuda, **State House**, is at the end of King Street. It was founded in 1620 by Governor Nathaniel Butler, who opted for an Italianate design, convinced Bermuda lay on the same latitude as Italy (*open*: most Wednesdays 10.00–16.00hrs). North of State House, a cenotaph in **Somers Gardens** commemorates brave Sir George, whose heart was buried here.

St George has several small and interesting museums. The **Historical Society Museum**, Kent Street, displays island artefacts and colonial furnishings in an 18th-century cottage; and the nearby **Featherbed Alley Printery** contains an antique working press. Eighteenth-century **St Peter's Church** was founded on the site of Bermuda's first wooden church, erected in 1612. It has a fascinating 300-year-old graveyard. Across York Street, the **Confederate Museum** dates from 1700. Its restored interior, once a Confederate agent's office, now houses Civil War era exhibits illustrating Bermuda's role as a one-time staging post for arms from Europe.

On Water Street, the **Carriage Museum** recalls island travel before the introduction of motor vehicles in 1946 with a collection of pony carts and splendid Victorian carriages. Diagonally across the street, the 1775 **Tucker House** once belonged to one of Bermuda's most important families, and is furnished with antique Bermudian cedar furniture, silver and paintings.

Carriage Museum open: Monday to Friday 10.00–17.00hrs.
Confederate Museum open: Monday to Saturday 10.00–16.00hrs (November to March 09.30–16.30hrs).
Deliverance open: Monday to Saturday 10.00–16.00hrs (December to March, Wednesday and Saturday only).
Featherbed Alley Printery open: Monday, Tuesday and Thursday to Saturday 10.00–16.00hrs; Wednesday 11.00–14.00hrs.

Tropical Anglican: St Peter's Church, St George

Tucker House open: Monday to Saturday 10.00–16.00hrs (April to October 09.30–16.30hrs).

Eating Out
Bermuda has a plethora of pubs. On Hamilton's Front Street, try **The Cock and Feather** (tel: 441/295 2263), or **Flanagan's Irish Pub** (tel: 441/295 8299) for affordable pub grub; while the **Harbourfront Restaurant** (tel: 441/295 4207) serves Mediterranean dishes, seafood and sushi. South of Hamilton, the elegant **Fourways Inn**, Paget (tel: 441/236 6517) offers outdoor dining and probably the best gourmet cuisine on the island. In the West End, **The Frog and Onion**, Royal Naval Dockyard (tel: 441/234 2900) is highly recommended for pub grub and seafood. In St George, sample fish and chips at **The Pub on the Square**, Kings Square (tel: 441/297 1522); or elect for the more genteel surroundings and 18th-century setting of **The Carriage House**, Water Street (tel: 441/297 1270).

OTHER CRUISING ISLANDS

CAYMAN ISLANDS

A trio of small, low-lying islands 150 miles (240km) south of Cuba, the Caymans lie poised on the brink of the Cayman Trench, a 25,000-foot (7,500m) trough at the deepest point of the Caribbean. The dusty, scrub-covered islands are the tips of sea mountains, and although the landscape is uninspiring above sea level, the Caymans offer spectacular underwater scenery.

The largest island, Grand Cayman, is the most developed, an offshore banking and insurance haven with a healthy tourist industry. Life on the diminutive islands of Cayman Brac and Little Cayman, some 90 miles (145km) northeast (frequent local flights), is lived at a distinctly slower pace, and they make an ideal destination for true escapist holidays.

Taking the time to drop in and meet with the locals at Stingray City, Grand Cayman

◆◆
GEORGE TOWN

The islands' capital is always a popular cruise ship destination largely due to its tax-free shopping status. Fort Street and the Kirk Freeport Plaza are magnets for the shop-till-you-drop crowd.

The quayside information kiosk distributes walk tour maps. For an introduction to island history, drop in at the **Cayman Islands National Museum** in the restored 1830s Old Courts Building. Among the nautical memorabilia and sections on seafaring traditions, there are descriptions of turtle hunting. *National Museum open*: Monday to Friday 09.30–17.30hrs; Saturday 10.00–16.00hrs.

CAYMAN TURTLE FARM
West Bay Road, north of George Town
At the only commercial green turtle farm in the world, visitors are invited to observe the lifecycle of a turtle from egg to 600-pound (270kg) leviathan, and then sample Cayman turtle cuisine. A small proportion of the thousands of turtles bred here annually are released into the wild.
Open: daily, 09.00–17.00hrs.

CAYMAN WALL
Diving the walls to the north and west of Grand Cayman is an experience not to be missed. These vertical underwater drops are clustered with corals and inhabited by a staggering variety of other marine life. For non-divers, **Atlantis Submarine** (tel: 345/949 7700) operate frequent mini-sub tours from George Town.

HELL
West Bay, north of George Town
A touristy enclave of souvenir shops and a post office has sprung up around a group of weird limestone rock formations dating back over a million years. Postcards sell like hot cakes and get post-marked from Hell.

SEVEN MILE BEACH
north of George Town
A spectacular sweep of powder-soft white sand, Seven Mile Beach (actually nearer 5½ miles/9km) is the main resort area, fringed by hotels, condominiums, restaurants, bars and watersports centres with snorkelling gear, windsurfers, jet-skis and sail boats for rent. (For a quiet beach, head for the island's East End or the snorkelling sites at Parrots Reef and Smiths Cove, south of George Town.)

STINGRAY CITY
North Sound
An amazing opportunity to swim with wild, but remarkably friendly stingrays in the sheltered waters of the North Sound. Some of these graceful creatures, which can measure up to 6 feet (1.8m) from wingtip to wingtip, will nibble fishy snacks from the hand and allow themselves to be petted. There are boat trips, too.

Eating Out
Seafood is very much the order of the day in Grand Cayman. In George Town, **The Cracked Conch**, Selkirk Plaza, is a lively bar and restaurant serving Cayman conch dishes. To the south, **Grand Old House**, South Church Street (tel: 345/949 9333) is renowned for continental cuisine served in a colonial house with a breezy occanside deck; while **Crow's Nest**, South Sound Road (tel: 345/949 9366) offers fine local cuisine with waterfront views. Heading north, there is seafood, Caribbean cooking and South Sea décor at **Almond Tree**, West Bay Road (tel: 345/949 2893); and right up on the north coast, **Ristorante Pappagallo**, Conch Point (tel: 345/949 1119) specialises in excellent Italian cuisine.

OTHER CRUISING ISLANDS

JAMAICA

Mountainous and beautiful Jamaica was called Xamayca (Land of Wood and Water) by Arawak Indians and Christopher Columbus described it as 'the fairest island that eyes have beheld'. The third-largest of the Caribbean islands at 4,411 square miles (11,425sq km), Jamaica's rich and varied terrain encompasses the heights of the Blue Mountains in the east, the craggy karst plateau of Cockpit Country in the west, lush forests and rushing rivers, and a necklace of superb north coast beaches harbouring the main tourist areas of Negril, Montego Bay and Ocho Rios.

Spanish colonists established the first settlement on the island in 1510, and the British captured Jamaica in 1655. They transformed it into one of the world's largest sugar producers until the abolition of slavery in 1834. Jamaica was the first British colony in the Caribbean to achieve full independence, in 1962, and the island is something of a cultural leader in the region, the birthplace of reggae and Rastafarianism.

◆

KINGSTON

Jamaica's south coast capital is the least tourist-orientated town on the island. However, a few cruise ships berth in the sheltered harbour and there are several low-key sights to enjoy. One is a ferry ride across to **Fort Charles** with views back to the Blue Mountains. During the 17th century this was the site of Port Royal, a piratical hellhole frequented by the likes of Henry Morgan and Edward Teach (aka Blackbeard) until it was swallowed up by the sea during a massive earthquake in 1692. In the downtown district, the **National Gallery of Jamaica** has one of the finest collections of Caribbean art in the region. Head north to Old Hope Road, for lovely **Devon House**, a restored 19th-century great house with craft shops in the old stables; the **Bob Marley Museum**, which honours the legendary Jamaican reggae star in the former Tuff Gong recording studio; and the exuberantly colourful **Hope Botanical Gardens** established in 1881. Within the gardens there is also a zoo.

Bob Marley Museum open: Monday, Tuesday, Thursday and Friday 09.00–17.00hrs; Wednesday and Saturday noon–18.00hrs.
Devon House open: Tuesday to Saturday 10.00–17.00hrs.
Hope Botanical Gardens open: daily, 08.30–18.30hrs.
National Gallery of Jamaica open: Monday to Saturday 10.00–17.00hrs.

◆

APPLETON ESTATE EXPRESS

departures from Montego Bay
An air-conditioned bus ride into the hills fetches up at the Appleton Estate rum distillery for a glimpse of the cane-crushers and boiling vats before sampling fresh-pressed cane juice, molasses and the finished product, Appleton Estate Rum, produced on the estate since 1745.
For opening schedules, tel: 809/963 2210.

In the distance, Jamaica's Blue Mountains live up to their name

◆◆
BLACK RIVER SAFARIS

southwest coast

In a quiet, undeveloped corner of the island, near the fishing village of Black River, safari boat rides depart from Salt Bridge four times a day for the Great Morass, a mangrove swamp area teeming with undisturbed wildlife from herons and egrets to basking crocodiles.

Open: daily. For schedules, tel: 809/965 2513.

◆◆◆
BLUE MOUNTAINS ✓

north of Kingston

Viewed from a distance, the mile-high (1,6km) peaks of Jamaica's eastern mountain range are indeed a hazy blue, but close up they are cloaked in a tangle of deep green forest jungle. It is a challenging hike to Blue Mountain Peak (7,395ft/ 2,254m), the highest point of the range, but two cross-island roads cut across the mountains north of Kingston: the main Route A3 to Annotto Bay, which passes the Castleton Botanic Gardens dating from 1862; and the twisting, beautiful Route B1 to Buff Bay. The latter climbs up past the Cinchona Gardens, 5,500 feet (1,675m) above sea level, with stunning views. There are several coffee factories along the way too. Both Mavis Bank and Silver Hill produce the aromatic Blue Mountain coffee beans which send *aficionados* into raptures.

◆◆◆
DUNN'S RIVER FALLS
2 miles (3km) west of Ocho Rios
A top island attraction, these deliciously cool mountain waterfalls tumble down a series of gentle ledges 600 feet (180m) through the forest to the coast. Guides lead 'daisy chains' of swimsuited visitors hand-in-hand up the slippery route to the top. There are changing rooms and lockers down on the beach.
Open: daily, 08.00–17.00hrs.

'Daisy chain' at Dunn's River

◆◆◆
FIREFLY
17 miles (27km) east of Ocho Rios
Playwright and composer Noel Coward's enviably positioned Jamaican retreat has been meticulously restored with personal memorabilia from manuscripts and star-spangled photographs to the great man's silk pyjamas. Coward's grave is in the gardens, 1,000 feet (300m) above the coast.
Open: Monday to Saturday 09.00–16.00hrs.

◆◆
GREENWOOD GREAT HOUSE
16 miles (25km) east of Montego Bay
A sturdy grey-stone mansion dating from the 1790s, Greenwood was built by plantation-owning relatives of the poet Elizabeth Barrett Browning. The antique-filled interior contains a collection of rare musical instruments, and a highlight is the view from the second-storey veranda.
Open: daily, 09.00–17.00hrs.

◆◆
MARTHA BRAE RAFTING
Rafters' Village, near Falmouth
A lazy river trip down the Martha Brae is an enjoyable way to view unspoilt tropical jungle, birds and butterflies. The trip takes 90 minutes, and the two-man bamboo rafts are poled downstream by local guides.
Raft trips: daily, 09.00–17.00hrs.

◆◆
MONTEGO BAY
northwest coast
Jamaica's tourist capital and second-largest town, Mo Bay, is

a good base for a wide variety of excursions. The city centre is **Sam Sharpe Square**, named after the leader of the 1831 slave rebellion whose statue watches over the street vendors and The Cage, a former slave lock-up. Towards the waterfront there is souvenir-hunting to be done at the **Craft Market**. The main shopping and entertainment district focuses on hotel-lined Gloucester Avenue, which heads north towards **Doctor's Cave Beach**. Once touted for its restorative properties, this is the most popular beach in town.

◆◆◆
NEGRIL
west coast
In what is by far the most appealing of Jamaica's tourist resort areas, no building can grow taller than a coconut palm.

Palm-thatched cabins with a view on the cliffs at Negril

The chief attraction here is the beaches, notably **Long Bay**'s 7-mile (11km) stretch of dazzling white sand; and spotless **Bloody Bay** where whalers once cleaned their catch. There are excellent watersports facilities.

◆◆
OCHO RIOS
central north coast
A modern resort centre and the island's chief cruise port, Ochi is well supplied with all the tourist necessities from shopping and dining to nightlife and watersports. There are several attractions close by, including historical and cultural exhibits at the **Cobaya Museum and Gardens**; and top quality craft shopping at **Harmony Hall**.

◆◆◆
PORT ANTONIO
northeast coast
Blessed by not one, but two stunning deepwater bays and

backed by the Blue Mountains, Port Antonio was a banana boat port and Jamaica's first resort around the turn of the century. During the 1940s and '50s it enjoyed a brief heyday as an exclusive Hollywood hideaway for the likes of Errol Flynn and Bette Davis. Today, mercifully undeveloped, the town is a quiet oasis with a smattering of Victorian buildings. Nearby sights include the turquoise waters of the Blue Hole; the Nonsuch Caves; and rafting on the Rio Grande.

PROSPECT PLANTATION
4 miles (6km) east of Ocho Rios
Bananas, coffee, cocoa, pineapples, coconuts and limes are grown on this 1,000-acre (405ha) working plantation. Wagon trips and horseback rides around the estate trundle off to the sugar cane fields, and stop at a dramatic lookout above the White River Gorge.
Open: daily tours at 10.30, 14.00 and 15.30hrs.

ROCKLAND BIRD SANCTUARY
8 miles (13km) south of Montego Bay
'Bird lady' Lisa Salmon first set up her bird feeding station in the forested highlands above Anchovy in 1958. Dozens of native and migrating birds drop in for an afternoon snack and some, such as red-billed streamertails, the tiny hummingbirds known as doctor birds (Jamaica's national symbol), will feed from hand-held bottles of sugar water.
Open: daily, 15.15–17.15hrs.

ROSE HALL GREAT HOUSE
10 miles (16km) east of Montego Bay
This is the grandest of Jamaica's great houses, built around 1770 and richly furnished with antiques. But despite the opulent surroundings of the Georgian house, the main topic of the guided tours is the legend of Annie Palmer, the White Witch of Rose Hall: the infamous 19th-century mistress of the house is said to have murdered three husbands and a string of slave lovers before meeting her own gory end.
Open: daily, 09.00–18.00hrs.

Eating Out
Kingston's **Devon House**, 26 Hope Road (tel: 809/929 7046) offers a choice of eateries. In Montego Bay, sample old colonial elegance and continental cuisine at **The Georgian House**, Orange Street (tel: 809/952 0632); seafood at **Marguerite's By The Sea**, Gloucester Avenue (tel: 809/952 4777); or genuine Jamaican jerk (barbecued meats, chicken and fish) at the **Pork Pit**, Gloucester Avenue. Good local food is served up in Negril at **Cosmo's**, Long Beach (tel: 809/957 4330). Ocho Rios dining options include the terrace at **Almond Tree**, Hibiscus Lodge, 83 Main Street (tel: 809/974 2676); Italian food at **Evita's**, Eden Bower Road (tel: 809/974 2333); or the **Jerk Centre**, Main Street. The best local restaurant in Port Antonio is **Daddy Dee**, West Street; for international cuisine, try the **Admiralty Club**, Navy Island (tel: 809/993 2667).

PUERTO RICO

Puerto Rico is the most easterly and smallest (100 miles by 35 miles/160km by 56km) of the Greater Antilles. From the rainforested heights of the Cordillera Central, the mountains drop sharply away to agricultural plains and a fringe of spectacular beaches. Columbus visited in 1493, but Puerto Rico was not settled until the arrival of Ponce de León, the discoverer of Florida, in 1508. The Spanish held the island for four centuries until it passed to the US after the Spanish-American War in 1898. A thousand miles (1,600km) southeast of Miami, Puerto Rico is a semi-autonomous commonwealth territory of the

Old San Juan fortress lookout

US, and the American influence is unavoidable in the main tourist areas, where both Spanish and English are commonly spoken. However, beyond the high-rise hotel enclaves, Puerto Rico's Spanish Catholic heritage is still widely evident in the 18th-century colonial architecture of Old San Juan, Spanish-style *fiestas* and Hispanic cuisine, even the time-honoured evening *paseo* (a pre-dinner stroll). Despite recent referenda and the obvious financial advantages, Puerto Ricans have so far rejected attempts to have their country adopted as the 51st State of the Union.

OTHER CRUISING ISLANDS

◆◆◆
SAN JUAN

The whole island was named after San Juan's *puerto rico* (rich port), and cruise passengers have a prime view of the huge sheltered bay overlooked by fortified Old San Juan and the vast, brooding El Morro fortress. The fast-growing modern city has sprawled out east to the high-rise beach suburb of Condado, where many visitors choose to stay. However, it is Old San Juan that everyone comes to enjoy, an utterly charming Spanish quarter of steep streets and *escalinatas* (flights of steps) lined by pastel pink, yellow, blue and green balconied townhouses. The best shopping is here too, and plenty of bars and restaurants.

On the sightseeing front, the 16th-century fortress of **San Felipe del Morro** (better known as El Morro), is not to be missed. Ponce de León's daughter and son-in-law built the original fortified house on the site of the **Casa Blanca** in 1521. The house is now a museum of family life in 16th- and 17th-century Puerto Rico. On Plaza de San José, the Ponce de León statue hails visitors to the 16th-century family church, **Iglesia de San José**. Seventeenth-century **Fort San Cristóbal**, guarding the Atlantic approaches to the old city, is also open for inspection.

Casa Blanca open: Tuesday to Sunday 09.00hrs–noon and 13.00–16.00hrs.
Fort San Cristóbal open: daily, 09.00–17.00hrs.
San Felipe del Morro open: daily, 08.00–18.00hrs.

◆◆◆
BOQUERÓN
southwest coast

One of the best known beaches on the island, this splendid sweep of sand backed by palm trees is very popular at weekends. There are cafés and cabin rentals in the small seaside resort town, watersports equipment hire on the beach, and the Cabo Rojo Wildlife Reserve in the coastal mangrove forest to the south.

◆◆
LUQUILLO BEACH
northeast coast

A magnificent Atlantic coast beach lapped by glassy turquoise water. No need for a picnic as there are stalls under the palm trees doing a brisk trade in piña coladas, seafood taco rolls and *alcapurrias* (fritters).

◆◆
PONCE
south coast, 70 miles (112km) from San Juan

Puerto Rico's second city was founded by Ponce de León's great-grandson in the late 17th century. Its heart is tree-shaded **Plaza las Delicias**, flanked by the 17th-century, neo-classical **Catedral Nuestra Señora de la Guadalupe** and the eye-catching red-and-black **Museo Parque de Bombas** (Fire Station Museum) dating from 1882. On Avenue Las Americas, the **Museo de Arte de Ponce** (Ponce Art Museum) contains probably the finest collection of Western art in the region; and a favourite visit is the **Museo Castillo Serrallés**, on El Vigía hill, an imposing Spanish Revival mansion, with lovely gardens, built for a sugar baron in the 1930s.

Museo de Arte de Ponce open: daily, 10.00–16.00hrs.
Museo Castillo Serrallés open: Wednesday to Sunday 10.00–16.30hrs.
Museo Parque de Bombas open: Monday and Wednesday to Friday 09.30–18.00hrs.

◆◆
RIO CAMUY CAVE PARK
Lares, northwest coast
A massive subterranean cave system has been hollowed out of the karst limestone by the River Camuy. Trams trundle down to the mouth of the Clara Cave where a footpath picks up the trail into an impressive cavern, 170 feet (270m) high, festooned with towering stalagmites and giant icicle-like stalactites.
Open: Wednesday to Sunday 08.00–16.00hrs.

◆◆◆
EL YUNQUE (CARIBBEAN NATIONAL FOREST)
Route 191, 40 miles (64km) southeast of San Juan
On average it rains 350 days of the year (more than 100 billion gallons, or 450 billion litres, of rainwater annually) in Puerto Rico's lush and spectacular rainforest jungle. Some 2,000 feet (600m) above sea level, El Yunque (The Anvil) is a rampant tangle of lianas, ferns and epiphytes crowned by 100-foot- (30m) high trees. Various trails depart from the visitor centre along paths edged by colourful hibiscus, wild

The eye-catching Fire Station Museum in Ponce

ginger and bromeliads. The colourful and rare Puerto Rican parrot is still found here; look for its brilliant green and blue plumage and red headmarkings. Also valuable but tiny are Coqui tree frogs.

Eating Out
In Old San Juan *tapas* bars, serving a wide variety of tasty snacks, make an inexpensive lunchtime option. For more substantial fare, there are Italian specialities at **Amadeus**, Calle San Sebastian (tel: 787/722 8635); seafood and good local cooking at the historic **La Mallorquina**, Calle San Justo (tel: 787/722 3261), established in 1848; or simple snacks and meals at bustling **La Bombonera**, Calle San Francisco, a favourite local café-restaurant.
For straightforward waterfront dining in Boqueron, look no further than **Ruicof**, a stroll from the beach. One of the better dining rooms in Ponce is **El Ancla**, Playa de Ponce (tel: 787/840 2450).

OTHER CRUISING ISLANDS

TRINIDAD AND TOBAGO

The twin-island nation at the southern tip of the Caribbean island chain, Trinidad and Tobago make an odd couple. Loud, boisterous, multicultural Trinidad is home to the cosmopolitan capital, Port of Spain, and the famous Carnival. Laid-back, rural Tobago is an escapist haven with a wild, forested heartland and low-key tourist industry centred on a handful of beautiful beaches. Broken off the South American mainland as recently as 10,000 years ago, Trinidad was claimed for Spain by Columbus in 1498. The island welcomed French planters in the 18th century, before passing to Britain in 1802. After the abolition of slavery, plantation owners replaced their African work force with East Indian indentured labourers, and descendants of these Africans and Indians now make up around 40 per cent of the population each.

PORT OF SPAIN

The teeming streets of Port of Spain reflect Trinidad's complex multicultural heritage. A modern city has sprung up amid a welter of West Indian gingerbread homes, British colonial piles, mosques, markets and the wide open spaces of **Queen's Park Savannah**. Here a collection of grandiose turn-of-the-century mansions have earned the nickname 'The Magnificent Seven', while the **Botanical Gardens** and **Emperor Valley Zoo** feature a fine array of tropical flora and fauna. For entertaining shopping head for the Indian markets and street stalls on Frederick Street, and there is island history and cultural exhibits at the **National Museum and Art Gallery**, at Frederick and Keate Streets.

National Museum open: Tuesday to Saturday 10.00–18.00hrs.
Zoo open: daily, 09.30–18.00hrs.

ASA WRIGHT NATURE CENTRE

Arima Valley, east of Port of Spain

Trinidad is an ornithologist's dream, but even the uninitiated can enjoy this trip up into the Northern Range rainforest. From the Centre, trails disappear off into the forest, and the famous birdlife is rivalled by exuberant flora and butterflies.

Open: daily, 09.00–17.00hrs.

CARONI BIRD SANCTUARY

8 miles (13km) south of Port of Spain

A 450-acre (180ha) marshland and mangrove swamp preserve, the sanctuary harbours around half the island's 300 bird species. The evening flight of scarlet ibis (from around 16.00hrs) is spectacular.

◆◆

FORT GEORGE

10 miles (16km) west of Port of Spain

Soon after the British took charge of the island they built this hilltop fortress to guard the approaches to Port of Spain. On a clear day, the sweeping views across the city and off to Venezuela are matchless.

Open: daily, 09.00–18.00hrs.

Maracas Bay

◆◆◆
MARACAS BAY
north coast
Take the Skyline Highway north from Port of Spain for a 35-minute scenic drive over the mountains to Trinidad's most famous beach, a stretch of powder-soft sand shaded by slanting palms.

◆
PITCH LAKE
southwest, near La Brea
It is said Sir Walter Raleigh caulked his ships with sticky pitch from this 90-acre (36ha) asphalt 'lake'. Visitors can walk on the edges of the world's largest asphalt deposit, which is around 300 feet (90m) deep at its centre, and is now mined for road building and roofing.

◆◆◆
TOBAGO
Cruise ships put into Tobago at **Scarborough**, the sleepy island capital overlooked by 18th-century **Fort King George**, now home to an arts centre and museum (*open*: Monday to Friday 09.00–17.00hrs). The town is divided into two parts with the harbour and Central Market on the lower level. The old colonial buildings, including the 1825 House of Assembly, are further uphill.

All tours of Tobago include the southern beach beauty spot of **Pigeon Point** bordering the **Buccoo Reef National Park** underwater preserve. The **Tobago Forest Reserve**, on the north coast, offers winding forest trails. Near Roxborough, guides lead hikes up to the **Argyll Waterfall**; and on the road to the pretty fishing village of **Speyside**, Tobago's highest waterfalls, the **King's Bay Falls**, tumble down into refreshing natural swimming holes.

Eating Out
Trinidadian cooking is an eclectic mish-mash of West Indian, Indian, French Creole and Chinese cuisine. A lively restaurant-bar, **Rafters**, 6 Warner Street (tel: 868/628 9258) serves seafood and local dishes. There is excellent French Creole cuisine in the Hotel Normandie's dining room, **La Fantaisie**, St Ann's (tel: 868/624 1181); Indian specialities at **Monsoon**, 72 Tragarete Road (tel: 868/628 7684); or Chinese at **Hong Kong City**, Tragarete and Maraval Roads (tel: 868/622 3949). On Tobago, Scarborough's finest is probably **The Old Donkey Cart Restaurant**, Bacolet Street (tel: 868/639 3551); and **Rouselle's**, Barcolet Street (tel: 868/639 4738) does great things with seafood. The **Black Rock Café**, Black Rock (tel: 868/639 7625) serves seafood and steaks out on the veranda.

Peace and Quiet

Wildlife and Countryside in the Caribbean by Paul Sterry

For those dreaming of a holiday with palm-fringed beaches, tropical seas and non-stop sunshine, the Caribbean islands are an ideal destination. Tens of thousands of holiday-makers find the lure of these stunning islands irresistible, and the beaches near tourist complexes are often crowded. Travel further afield and deserted coves can be found, while offshore are some of the finest coral reefs in the world waiting to be discovered. Coastal swamps and mangroves are home to vast numbers of wetland birds which in turn feed on the abundance of invertebrate and fish life found there.

The interior terrain of the islands varies considerably in character along the island chain of the Caribbean. On some there are lush tropical rainforests while on others arid, desert-like habitats are dominated by large and imposing cacti. The evidence of human influence on the environment is everywhere to be seen. Although this often takes the form of clearance of forest for agriculture, the cultivated land –

The scarlet ibis is a native of Trinidad's Caroni Swamp

and the secondary forest that develops after it has been abandoned – is not without wildlife interest either. Almost any corner of the Caribbean with natural or semi-natural vegetation is likely to be good for wildlife, but the following areas merit particular attention.

Morne Trois Pitons National Park, Dominica
See also page 17.
Birdwatching is good but many species can be rather unobtrusive amid the shade cast by the lush rainforest vegetation despite their bright colours.

Grand Etang Forest Reserve, Grenada
See page 20 for details.

Rainforest Walk, St Lucia
Remaining areas of St Lucia's magnificent rainforest are protected within the Edmund and Quillesse Forest Reserves on the south-central part of the island. Perhaps the best way to explore the area, with a chance to observe the rare St Lucia parrot, is to take the Rainforest Walk between the villages of Fond St Jacques and Mahaut.

PEACE AND QUIET

Left to right: *Bahama yellowthroat;
diving sea turtle; Cayman parrot;
Spectacled caiman; Green-throated
carib; Cook's tree boa*

Buccament Forest Nature Trail, St Vincent

A short way to the north of
Kingstown, an excellent nature
trail starts at the head of the
Buccament Valley and winds
along the slopes of Grand
Bonhomme mountain. Imposing
giant hardwoods, tree ferns and
strangler figs add stature to the
scenery and the birdlife includes
the rare St Vincent parrot.

Caul's Pond, Anguilla

A short distance southeast from
East End Village lies a coastal
pool known as Caul's Pond.
Large numbers of birds roost
here and the brackish waters
harbour food for species such as
black-necked stilts. The greatest
range of birdlife can be found
during the autumn when migrant
waders from North America
pass through on their southward
migration. Throughout the year,
watch out for herons, egrets and
white-cheeked pintails.

Great Bird Island, Antigua

Uninhabited Great Bird Island
lies just off the northwest coast of

Seabirds

The offshore waters of the
Caribbean are rich in marine
life and support large numbers
of seabirds which often breed
on isolated islets or protected
beaches. Their numbers
include red-billed tropicbirds,
sooty terns, brown boobies and
magnificent frigatebirds.

Antigua and can be reached by
boat charters from the main
island. It is best visited between
March and September when the
colonies of seabirds are
breeding.
Look out in particular for red-
billed tropicbirds, sooty terns
and common noddies.

Great Salt Pond, St Kitts

This large, shallow pool lies in
the far southeast of the island
and is close to sea on three
sides. It is of greatest interest to
birdwatchers between August
and October when North
American waders, gulls and
terns stop off on their southward
autumn migration. Some remain
throughout the winter and
numbers are augmented again
in spring when birds pass
through on their return journeys
northwards.

The Baths, Virgin Gorda, British Virgin Islands

The Baths comprise a jumble of massive boulders which create pools and crashing surf. They are in the southwest of the island, not far from Devil's Bay National Park, an isolated sandy beach at the tip of the island.

Rainforest, St Croix, US Virgin Islands

Tropical forest cloaks the northwest corner of St Croix and can be explored by driving the network of roads that head north and east from Frederiksted. Magnificent trees are festooned with epiphytic plants, and birds can be found among the shady foliage and on the forest floor.

Sandy Point National Wildlife Refuge, St Croix, US Virgin Islands

At the far southwestern tip of St Croix, Sandy Point attracts numerous seabirds offshore, but the site is best known as a breeding ground for leatherback, green and hawksbill turtles which lay their eggs in the sand beach.

Virgin Islands National Park, St John, US Virgin Islands

See page 44 for details.

Snorkelling

For both diving enthusiasts and the more casual snorkelling visitors, many of the Caribbean islands offer fantastic opportunities for underwater exploration. The coral reefs that fringe many of the islands are home to colourful fish and invertebrates and the warm waters allow this pursuit to be indulged at length.

The Cayman Islands, St Lucia and Antigua are all renowned for their diving and snorkelling possibilities.

Guadeloupe National Park

See page 51 for details.

Caravelle Peninsula, Martinique

Facing the brunt of Atlantic gales on Martinique's northeast coast, this promontory is protected by nature reserve status and is part of the Regional Natural Park of Martinique. Tropical forests and mangroves are dominant, seabirds can be seen offshore, and waders, herons and gulls linger on the shores, especially from late summer to early winter.

Christoffel National Park, Curaçao

See page 63 for details.

PEACE AND QUIET

Caribbean National Forest, Puerto Rico

See also page 95.
Also known as El Yunque, this area of rainforest dominates the eastern tip of Puerto Rico. The park can be reached by road from the highway that runs from San Juan to Luquillo and trails allow exploration on foot.

Graeme Hall Swamp, Barbados

This mangrove-fringed site lies a short distance from Bridgetown in the southeast of the island. Resident water birds, which include herons and egrets, are joined in autumn by migrant waders from North America.

Blue Mountains, Jamaica

See also pages 89–90.
The dominating peaks of eastern Jamaica can be explored by taking one of the many trails between Newcastle and Hardwar Gap. Luxuriant vegetation can be found growing beneath the often majestic trees.

Caroni Bird Sanctuary, Trinidad

This splendid area of mangrove

Humpback whale tail fluke

> **Scarlet Ibis**
> Trinidad's national bird is also its most colourful and gaudy. As with flamingos, the ibis' colour is derived from its food, which includes shrimps and prawns. Its days are spent probing in shallow water using its long, down-curved bill; at night the birds roost communally in trees. In Trinidad, Caroni Swamp is their most important sanctuary.

swamp is the roosting site for numerous scarlet ibis which can be observed from boat tours as the birds arrive at dusk. Large numbers of other wetland birds also occur, along with alligator-like spectacled caimans.

Asa Wright Nature Centre, Trinidad

See also page 96.
This private reserve, set amid the rainforest, is a birdwatcher's paradise; it lies in the north of the island, not far from Arima. On numerous trails, visitors can see forest birds including hummingbirds, toucans, motmots and parrots. An impressive range of birds can also be seen from the hotel veranda.

> **Humpback Whale**
> Each year, humpback whales which have spent the summer months feeding off the coasts of Newfoundland and New England, move south to breed in the warm waters that bathe the Caribbean Islands. The best place to see them is often from the south coast of Bermuda as they pass by from March to May.

Practical

This section includes information on food, drink, shopping, accommodation, nightlife, tight budget, special events, etc.

FOOD AND DRINK

Caribbean cooking is generally simple and unpretentious. Staple foods such as rice 'n' peas (the 'peas' are red kidney beans), spinach-like callaloo soup, fresh fish and a wide variety of cheap and filling root vegetables, plantains and breadfruit are found throughout the islands. Caribbean markets are also piled high with bananas, pineapples, mangoes, guavas, papaya, soursop (transformed into fabulous ice cream) and the green, pine cone-shaped sugar apple. However, culinary traditions vary from island to island and the combination of influences – African, British, French, Dutch, Indian, Spanish or South American – produces variations from hearty platters of Jamaican jerk (meat and fish cooked in barbecue pits) to the more refined gourmet dishes of French Creole cuisine (see box, page 55).
The French islands of Guadeloupe and Martinique take good food very seriously, and Guadeloupe's annual Fête des Cuisinières, when the

Spicy Jamaican jerk pork and fresh coconut milk

island's best female chefs gather for a major cook-out every August, is one of the biggest events in the local calendar. Adventurous gourmets will find another traditionally French culinary speciality served in

FOOD AND DRINK

Rich Blue Mountain flavour in a Jamaican coffee liqueur

Dominica, where 'mountain chicken' (frogs' legs) is considered a local delicacy. No visit to Barbados would be complete without sampling a flying fish sandwich. Bajans and their Windward Island neighbours are also very keen on pepperpot, a spicy meat stew, and lashings of hot sauce. No decent local restaurant in the region fails to place a bottle of this incendiary red or sometimes yellow (coloured with turmeric) brew on the table.

Trinidad is justly celebrated for its eclectic national cuisine which has been heavily influenced by the East Indian and Chinese migrants. Indian-style snacks, such as *roti* (chapati envelopes filled with curried meat or vegetables) and doubles (with a spicy, chick pea filling), are favourite items in the local fast food pantheon, and Port of Spain is well served by Chinese restaurants.

Snacking in Puerto Rico is also highly recommended, although the primary influence here is Spanish. Abandon the American fast food chains and bland international hotel cuisine for *alcapurrias* (savoury or sweet fritters), *empanadas* (meat- or vegetable-filled pastry pockets), tasty *picadillos* (the local variation on a hamburger), and *arroz con pollo* (a Caribbean-influenced rice and chicken dish cooked in coconut milk).

Drink

Whether it be dark, light, spiced or mixed into sweet, creamy liqueur-type concoctions, rum is the favourite tipple throughout the Caribbean region. Traditionally, the best rums are the dark rums from Barbados and Jamaica, but Puerto Rico with Bacardi and St Croix with Cruzan are renowned for white rums, while most of the islands produce their own brew. The Caribbean cocktail hour, long on punches, piña coladas and exotic fruit-flavoured daiquiris, is a homage to the versatility of local rum.

As no wine is produced in the region it has to be imported, a fact reflected in the price. But there are good local beers, such as Carib, Jamaica's Red Stripe, and Banks in Barbados. Non-alcoholic drinks include a bevy of delicious, fresh fruit juices, coconut milk, and sugar cane juice.

SHOPPING

Hot on the heels of sunbathing and relaxing, shopping is one of the top attractions for visitors to the Caribbean. Cruise passengers, in particular, are renowned for their high-spending ways in the duty-free ports of Bermuda, Grand Cayman, St Barts, Sint Maarten and St Thomas, and many cruise ship facilities on other islands offer duty-free shopping at the foot of the gangplank.

The tempting array of imported luxury goods comes from around the world and, in some cases, prices can represent a saving of 25 to 50 per cent on US retail prices. Top-brand Japanese cameras, French perfumes, fine liquors, watches and diamond jewellery are among the best sellers, also British china, crystal and woollens, the latter making a popular if unlikely buy in the tropical climate. The best bargains are usually found among fashionable items, such as the latest camera or watch, inspiring cut-throat competition between local traders and spelling good news for buyers prepared to shop around a bit. Most shops are happy to accept major credit cards, US dollar travellers' cheques or cash. However, duty-free shopping does not always deliver all it promises. Before making any major purchases, it is sensible to know prices back home and ensure that the duty-free 'bargain' does not turn into a liability when you are faced with a hefty import duty bill at the end of the holiday.

Jewellery makes an inexpensive and easy-to-pack souvenir

Shopping Around the Islands

A popular shopping stop for many visitors is the local straw market. The village of Corossol on St Barts is famous for its intricate straw work and traditional Carib Indian basketwork is a speciality of Dominica, but for most visitors the straw market is a chance to stock up on beach necessities from straw hats and woven mats to colourful baskets and cheap T-shirts. Bargaining is expected

SHOPPING

in Nassau's famous Straw Market, and most islands have their own (if slightly less overwhelming) version, or a craft market selling simple and inexpensive local souvenirs. For more upmarket Caribbean crafts, there are a number of galleries selling original paintings and prints on Philipsburg's Front Street in Sint Maarten; while Tillet Gardens, at Anna's Retreat in St Thomas, is a pleasant artists' enclave. Another excellent source of island crafts is Harmony Hall, with outposts in Antigua (see page 31), and just outside Ocho Rios in Jamaica. They are particularly good on contemporary paintings by local

Basket-weaving in the market

and Haïtian artists, pottery and sculpture. The Best of Barbados souvenir shop chain is also a reputable source of local crafts, gifts, jewellery and Caribbean cookbooks.

Colourful printed cottons make another great Caribbean souvenir idea. Caribelle Batik in St Kitt's and Bagshaw Studios in St Lucia both welcome visitors to their studios and few leave empty-handed. Many boutiques sell unique silk-screened or hand-painted fabrics and T-shirts, and there are several local resort-wear labels to look out for such as BASE on Antigua. A useful tip for visitors to Guadeloupe and Martinique: pay by travellers' cheque and be rewarded with a 20 per cent discount on French luxury goods. Local rum is also a good buy here, and antiques lovers may find a few French colonial knick-knacks to take home.

In Trinidad, calypso and Carnival road march tapes feature high on many shopping lists. The best place to find them is Frederick Street in Port of Spain. Jamaica is the home of reggae, and also Blue Mountain coffee which is notably light and easy to pack. In Jamaica's Montego Bay and Ocho Rios, dedicated shoppers might prefer to leave the loud and pushy craft markets to browsers and head for shopping malls such as Overton Plaza and Westgate Plaza in Mo Bay, and Island Plaza in Ocho Rios.

Shopping Hours
Opening times vary throughout the region, and from shop to shop. (See page 119.)

ACCOMMODATION

Beach hotels and plantation retreats, all-inclusive resorts and self-catering apartments – the Caribbean offers plenty of choice on the accommodation front. It also has two distinct seasons. High-season rates apply from mid-December through to mid-April; during summer prices drop dramatically. In October and November, when most rain falls, many hotels close for refurbishment and staff holidays. No overall hotel classification system exists for the region, so major tour operators and their brochures are the best guide to what represents two-, three-, four- or five-star accommodation in European and American terms. Cruise-stay packages arranged from home will nominate a range of hotel options in establishments checked out by the tour operator. Independent travellers can obtain accommodation information from local tourist offices and their overseas representatives, or talk to a knowledgeable travel agent. It is important to note that local government taxes can add significantly to the basic room rate.

The top end of the Caribbean hotel scene is expensive and

Gracious living and tables on the veranda at the Rawlins Plantation Hotel, St Kitts

luxurious. Barbados is something of a leader in this field with a clutch of the most reputable and longest-established Caribbean beach hotels occupying prime positions along the leeward shore, nicknamed 'The Platinum Coast'. In the Grenadines, another luxury leader is exclusive Mustique where most guests stay in fully-staffed villas; and Virgin Gorda, in the British Virgin Islands, has several chic resorts. Other ex-British islands, notably St Kitts, Nevis, and Jamaica, are famous for their plantation hotels set in restored 17th- to 19th-century great houses, which are long on style, though usually inland from the beach.

Most islands boast a few attractive and comfortable inns and guest houses in the mid-price bracket. The ex-British islands score well again here, and the French islands contribute delightful *gîtes* (fully-furnished and equipped self-catering accommodation in villas or apartments outside town) and *relais créoles*, inns set in old Creole houses.

For visitors keen to keep a tight grip on their budget, all-inclusive resorts are an increasingly popular option, though many limit their intake to couples only, aged 18 or over. These resorts charge a one-off price which covers all meals, drinks, watersports, entertainments, local transportation and many other extras. All-inclusives are well-developed on Jamaica, St Lucia and Antigua. Jamaica is also renowned for its family resorts.

NIGHTLIFE

When the sun goes down, the action switches from the beach to the bar and, more often than not, there is Happy Hour to kick off the evening's entertainment. Caribbean nightlife veers from packed and friendly pub discos and impromptu jump-ups (parties) to dinner-dances and shows in some of the larger hotels. Local tourist office brochures list upcoming events and pubs and bars offering regular night-time entertainments. The hotel concierge should also be a good source of information on what's happening and where. Pubs, bars and barbecue nights on the beach are a good place to

Local dancers in Tobago

find live music. Check the calendar for calypso competitions, and for Carnival time or the summer season cropover festivals when the streets are transformed into one big jump-up with reggae singers, calypsonians and steel bands out partying with the dancers pretty much all night long.

Cruise ships import their own nightlife, offering a range of entertainments from Las Vegas-style all-singing-all-dancing shows to cabaret performances, discotheques, piano bars and casinos. Younger passengers on the party ships will also find some pretty wild games, competitions and the inevitable limbo dancing.

WEATHER AND WHEN TO GO

The Caribbean region lies in the tropics, so temperatures are fairly consistent throughout the year and the heat is generally tempered by cooling trade winds. Daytime temperatures average 78–86°F (26–30°C); while night-time temperatures average 59–64°F (15–18°C). The driest time of the year (and the most popular with visitors) is December to April. May/June and October/November tend to be the wettest months with a fair amount of cloud in between tropical showers, though showers occur year-round in rainforested areas. Hurricanes are a rarity, but most likely to occur in August/September. A thousand miles (1,600km) to the north, Bermuda is semi-tropical with definable seasons. Cruise ships only visit the island from April to October. At the height of summer (July/August), temperatures average 80°F (28°C).

Contentment on a Caribbean island cruise

CRUISE SHIPS

Cruising is, perhaps, the ultimate form of travel in the Caribbean region, combining maximum sightseeing opportunities with minimum hassle. As the world's number one cruise destination, it is visited by as many as 150 cruise ships offering tremendous scope to passengers. To make the most of cruising in the Caribbean, it is important to select the right type of cruise ship, whether it be one of the huge 2,000-passenger party ships aimed at the younger and cheaper end of the market, or a supremely elegant, deluxe vessel catering for a mere 50 to 100 discerning travellers.

The majority of the cruise ships operating in the Caribbean fall between these two extremes. Premium cruise vessels, staffed by experienced and well-trained crews, enjoy a high standard of accommodation, dining and facilities, including casinos and a range of entertainments and nightlife. They also tend to feature a couple of formal evenings when guests get to dress up in their full finery. Standard vessels generally appeal to a more casual crowd, and offer fewer facilities and smaller cabins.

There are a few sail-cruise ships plying the Caribbean. Though these are technically full-rigged, true sailing types should check how much time is actually spent sailing and how much under power. An advantage of these smaller vessels (150 to 400 passengers) is that they can call at a number of ports which are

Cruise ships in St Thomas, USVI

inaccessible to larger vessels. When choosing a cruise ship, always check that the facilities are suitable and the range of entertainments on offer is appealing. For instance, parents travelling with children should find out about children's activity programmes. There should be a choice of shore excursions at every port, and some cruise ships offer themed cruises with a cultural, educational or sporting element.

Most Caribbean cruises depart from Florida – Miami or Fort Lauderdale. San Juan, Puerto Rico, is also a major embarkation point. Cruises to Bermuda originate in New York or Boston. Another option is the cruise-stay holiday which combines a week's cruise with a week in a hotel. This sector of the market is gaining in popularity all the time.

HOW TO BE A LOCAL

They say there are 90 minutes in every Caribbean hour, so the first thing to remember is nothing is going to happen in a hurry. Island life is slow and easy, and even in town there is always time to exchange a civil greeting, have a chat about family and friends, and hang out, so relax and enjoy.

On the other hand, the gaggle of shouting, waving taxi drivers at the foot of the cruise ship gangplank or the high pressure hawkers in the market and on the beach can seem somewhat intimidating. The best escape is a smile and a firm 'no thank you'.

On the whole, Caribbean islanders are open and friendly towards visitors. They appreciate tourists who step off the beaten track and dine out in local restaurants (many have been badly hit by the all-inclusive resort scene); anybody is a welcome addition to jump-ups at Carnival and festival times; and the market ladies have a huge giggle explaining all the strange fruits, vegetables and spices to curious browsers. Expect to be the butt of numerous incomprehensible jokes. However, there are certain areas where islanders go to escape the tourists, and visitors should avoid them without a local host in tow.

Religion is still an important part of life for many islanders, and so is old-fashioned courtesy; stop to say hello before asking a question. Beachwear is not considered appropriate in town. Topless bathing is forbidden on all but the French islands, though in practice there are secluded beaches on most islands where it is acceptable.

CHILDREN

Cruises are one of the best options for parents travelling with children in the Caribbean. On the top family-orientated cruise ships, varied and entertaining activity programmes are available to junior cruisers aged 3 to 17. There are special meals, cots, baby-sitting facilities, and a further incentive in the raft of excellent discounts designed to lure the whole family aboard. Many hotels also offer children's activities, particularly in the school holidays, and while some islands are rather limited on the junior sightseeing scene, older children will enjoy the watersports, riding and tennis. It is vital to protect children from the baking Caribbean sun. Hats and lots of high-factor sunscreen are essential, and make sure they have plenty to drink.

TIGHT BUDGET

Budget travellers have their work cut out for them in the Caribbean. There is a general understanding that visitors have money, and requests at the tourist office for cheap accommodation, for instance, are greeted with surprise and a degree of disfavour.

● West Indian guest houses do exist in every major town, and although the accommodation is basic, it is cheap and friendly. On most islands the local police have to grant permission for camping.
● Local restaurants represent a good deal for the budget traveller, and beach bars serve cheap, cheerful and filling fast food. Shop in the markets for fresh fruit and vegetables.
● Local minibus services are very inexpensive, but do not expect a timetable. They leave when they are full.
● Ferries offer affordable island-hopping in the Virgin Islands, and the mailboat down through the Grenadines is a bargain.
● For a month's island-hopping, the local airlines LIAT and BWIA both offer excellent value multi-destination tickets with unlimited stops in one direction.

SPECIAL EVENTS

The Caribbean calendar is packed with special events from Carnival and Independence celebrations to regattas and arts festivals. As dates and venues can change from year to year, check with the local tourist office for full details. Listed below are just a fraction of the most lively events.

January
St Lucia's **New Year Festival** continues into January; Puerto Rico celebrates **Three Kings Day** on Epiphany; and St Barts hosts a **Music Festival**.

February
This is **Carnival** month with huge celebrations kicking off in Trinidad, Guadeloupe, Martinique, St Barts, St Lucia and Sint Maarten/Saint-Martin.

March
Montserrat, the Emerald Isle, celebrates **St Patrick's Day**.

April
Antigua's **Race Week**; St Thomas (USVI) celebrates **Carnival**.

May
The **Caribbean Jazz Festival** in Barbados; and a **Food Festival** in Sint Maarten/Saint-Martin.

June
Carnivals in the Grenadines; **Million Dollar Month**, sport fishing competitions in the Cayman Islands; **windsurfing regattas** in the Virgin Islands.

July
The month-long **Cropover** end of harvest festivities hit Barbados; Guadeloupe and Martinique celebrate **Bastille Day**; and Jamaica hosts **Reggae Sunsplash**.

August
Carnival in Anguilla and Grenada; the Nevis **Culturama Festival**; and St Barts celebrates its **Saint's Day**.

September
Muslim **Hosein Festival** in Trinidad; **St John Carnival**, US Virgin Islands.

October
Divali, the Hindu **Festival of Lights**, in Trinidad.

November
Independence celebrations in Barbados and Dominica; **Concordia Day** celebrating French-Dutch accord in Sint Maarten/Saint-Martin.

December
Christmas is celebrated big time in the Islands. St Vincent's **Nine Mornings** festivities lead up to 25 December; **Junkanoo** festivities in the Bahamas; **Carnival** in St Kitts and Nevis.

Bahamanian Junkanoo reveller

SPORT

The Caribbean is a Mecca for **watersports** enthusiasts. There is some of the finest **diving** in the world off the Cayman Islands, the Dutch Leeward Islands and the Bahamas, and most islands offer good **snorkelling**. The Grenadines, Virgin Islands, Antigua and St Barts are top **sailing** destinations. **Sport fishing** is a big draw in the Cayman Islands and Bahamas.

On land, **hiking** in the rainforests is increasingly popular, as is **horseback riding**. **Golf** courses are proliferating and almost every resort in the region has at least one **tennis** court.

Directory

This section contains day-to-day information, including travel, health, documentation, money matters and language tips

Contents

Arriving
Camping
Car Rental
Crime
Customs
  Regulations
Driving
Electricity
Embassies and
  Consulates

Emergency
  Telephone
  Numbers
Health
Holidays
Lost Property
Media
Money Matters
Opening Times
Pharmacies
Places of Worship
Police

Post Office
Public Transport
Student and Youth
  Travel
Telephones
Time
Tipping
Toilets
Tourist Offices
Visitors with
  Disabilities

Arriving

International flights serve a number of major Caribbean destinations; the most popular receive both scheduled and discounted charter flights. There is an extensive network of frequent inter-island air services giving access to the smaller islands.

Documentation

A valid passport is sufficient for entry to most Caribbean islands. US and Canadian visitors need only provide proof of identity in

Proudly presenting the catch of the day for inspection in Jamaica

the form of a driver's licence or voter registration card. Local immigration forms (distributed by the airline) should also be completed and will be collected on arrival.

Non-US visitors to the US Virgin Islands and Puerto Rico have to comply with US immigration requirements. British passport holders and other nationals participating in the US Visa Waiver programme will need to supply a completed visa waiver form (available from the airline check-in) on arrival. The accommodation section of this form must be completed, or entry may be refused.

Cruise ship passengers will complete immigration formalities on board.

Ground Transport and Information

Most Caribbean airports have an information desk providing hotel and public transport information. If there is no hotel shuttle, taxis are often the sole onward transport option, but they are plentiful, and the information desk can supply fare details.

Departure Tax

Many islands levy a departure tax payable at the flight check-in. The actual amount varies from island to island, but EC$25 (US$10) is the norm.

Camping

Camping is not encouraged in the Caribbean. Only the French Antilles and the Virgin Islands have approved campsites. On other islands it is neccessary to apply for police permission which is rarely granted.

Adventures accommodated

Car Rental

Car rental is readily available on most islands, but there are no hire cars on Bermuda. Rental cars are not cheap, and several islands also require visitors to purchase a temporary local driver's licence (available from the rental company or the local police station). Major car rental companies, such as Avis, Budget and Thrifty operate on several of the larger islands. There are also numerous local rental companies, but although they may appear to offer better deals, check insurance documents with care. Often the driver is held responsible for the first US$1,000 of any damage done to the vehicle, so think twice before bouncing off down some dirt track to a secluded beach. (See also **Driving**.)

Crime

Violent crime, particularly against tourists, is a rarity in the smaller islands. In more developed areas, such as Jamaica, St Thomas and Trinidad, avoid unlit backstreets and the beach after dark. Petty theft is a universal problem, so keep a close grip on handbags and cameras, lock rental cars, and keep valuables in the hotel or cabin safe.

Customs Regulations

Alcohol and tobacco allowances vary from island to island. As a rule, the limit stands at one litre of spirits and 200 cigarettes for every adult (aged 18 and over).

Driving

Some islands drive on the right, some on the left, but most islanders seem blissfully unaware that it makes any difference. Nobody drives very fast in the Caribbean as roads tend to be pretty rough with truly impressive potholes in places. Drivers are liable to stop for a chat on blind corners, goats and other livestock nap on the road, and children are apt to shoot out from the kerb in hot pursuit of footballs or each other.

The first rule of driving in the islands is take it very slowly and leave plenty of time. Before setting out, make sure the car is topped up with fuel, as petrol stations are few and far between outside town. Also, check the rental company has provided an emergency telephone number in the event of a breakdown.

Electricity

The electricity supply on most islands is 220 volts. In the US Virgin Islands (as in the mainland US) and Aruba, it is 110 volts. Some islands are running both, so check with the hotel before plugging in electrical equipment.

Embassies and Consulates

Every island state or principal island of a group, for example St Kitts, will have an embassy or consulate representing the interests of its most common visitor nationals.

Emergency Telephone Numbers

Each island has its own emergency telephone numbers for the police and ambulance services. It is advisable to check the relevant numbers on arrival. Numbers are also listed in local tourist information brochures; pick one up before leaving town.

Health

No inoculations or vaccinations are required to visit the Caribbean. However, immunisation against typhoid, polio and tetanus is recommended. AIDS is also present.

Tapwater is drinkable on most islands, but it is wise to buy bottled water and avoid iced drinks in less developed areas. Coral cuts are easily infected, so take care when diving. And be on the lookout for spiky sea urchins and jellyfish. Sensible hikers carry plenty of mosquito repellent for trips into the rainforest. High-factor sunscreen is a must for the first few days of Caribbean sun and on boat trips.

Hotels will arrange for a doctor's visit and cruise vessels all carry a ship's medical officer. Hospital facilities are generally good, but emergency cases on smaller islands may need to be airlifted to a major hospital.

Proper health insurance is essential – particularly on the American islands, where health care is very expensive. Travellers on medication should ensure they have an adequate supply of their prescribed medicine before leaving home.

Holidays

All banks, post offices, government and public offices, and most shops close on public holidays such as Christmas Day, Boxing Day, New Year's Day and Easter. The dates of other public holidays, including Carnival and annual Independence Day celebrations, vary from island to island. Information is available from the tourist office and local hotels.

Lost Property

Lost or stolen property should be reported to the nearest police station and a report obtained to substantiate any insurance claim. It is also worth checking with hotels in the vicinity in case the missing item has been handed in.

Media

Most islands have at least one daily newspaper carrying some international news, and American periodicals are available at many news-stands. Local radio and television channels are increasingly augmented with US-style cable networks. Cruise ships have satellite access to mainland US cable news.

Money Matters

The US dollar is local currency in Puerto Rico, the US and British Virgin Islands, and is accepted with alacrity throughout the region, though change will probably be given in local currency.

The ex-British Windward and Leeward Island states go with the Eastern Caribbean dollar (EC$) which has a fixed rate of exchange against the US dollar, as has the Bermuda dollar (BD$), and the Trinidad and Tobago dollar (TT$). The Bahamanian dollar is kept at parity with the US$; the Jamaican dollar (JM$) fluctuates. The French franc is used in the French Antilles; the Netherlands Antilles guilder in the Netherlands Antilles.

It is unwise to carry large amounts of cash, so US dollar travellers' cheques are a worthwhile investment. They are widely accepted in hotels, more expensive restaurants, and for larger purchases in tourist shops. There are banks on all the islands, but banking hours vary, service can be slow, and few banks offer ATM cashpoint facilities. Major credit cards are accepted at most tourist hotels and restaurants, but check in advance.

Opening Times

Caribbean opening times are very flexible, and occasionally frustrating for visitors. In main towns and tourist areas, offices are generally open Monday to

A Hindu temple in Trinidad

Friday from 08.00 or 08.30hrs to
16.00 or 16.30hrs with a
lunchtime break. Banking hours
are approximately Monday to
Friday 08.00hrs–noon and
13.00–15.00hrs, though some
may open longer on Fridays.
Shops are open Monday to
Friday 08.00–16.00hrs with a
lunch break, and Saturday
08.00–13.00hrs, closed Sundays.
However, tourist shops and
stores, particularly those in
cruise ship destinations, may
open later, stay open later, and
do business on Saturday
afternoons and Sundays.
Sightseeing attractions are often
a law unto themselves. Smaller,
less visited sights may not
bother to open if business looks
slow in the off-season, despite
the hours posted on the
entrance.

Pharmacies
Main towns are well supplied
with pharmacies carrying
familiar US brand-name drugs
and toiletries, but check the date
stamps on goods before
purchasing. For minor ailments,
there is usually a trained
pharmacist on hand to advise.
After normal shopping hours,
any pharmaceutical problems
have to be taken to the nearest
hospital or doctor.

Places of Worship
Christianity still has a strong hold
on the Caribbean and the region
is a prime target for US-based
evangelical sects. Most islands
offer a choice of Anglican, Baptist,
Methodist and Catholic churches
which welcome visitors. There
are also Muslim mosques and
Hindu temples in Trinidad, and
Jewish worshippers will find a
few synagogues.

Police
On the whole, local police are helpful and polite to visitors, assisting with directions and completing theft reports.

Post Office
Post offices are generally open Monday to Thursday 08.00–15.30hrs and Friday 08.00–16.30hrs; some may open on Saturday mornings. Inter-island mail services are slow; international post is even slower, so it is common to arrive home several weeks before the postcards turn up. However, stamp collectors are always keen to receive the unusual and colourful stamps produced around the region.

Taking the bus is an inexpensive way of exploring the islands

Public Transport

Buses
Public transport island-style is generally an inexpensive but fairly erratic bus service, and privately operated minibuses which make regular but unscheduled departures from the town centre to various destinations on demand.

Ferries
Inexpensive ferry services ply several routes around the US and British Virgin Islands. There are ferries between Anguilla and Sint Maarten/St-Martin; Sint Maarten/St-Martin and St Barts, Saba and Sint Eustatius; St Kitts and Nevis. In the Windward Islands, ferries link Guadeloupe, Dominica, Martinique and St Lucia; Grenada, Carriacou and Petit

Martinique; and there are several departures daily from St Vincent to Bequia, while other ferries, plus the mailboat, provide services down the Grenadines.

Taxis

Visitors tend to prefer taxis which can be picked up at the airport or cruise ship dock or arranged by the hotel. Taxi fares are fixed and rates are posted at the airport and tourist office. They are usually quoted in both US dollars and local currency. Always agree the rate with the driver before setting off.

Student and Youth Travel

The Caribbean is not geared towards budget travellers (see **Tight Budget**, page 112). Foreign student cards may secure a small reduction in admission to local attractions, but there is no guarantee.

Telephones

The Caribbean telephone network is generally efficient and easy to use. There are plenty of public telephones which accept both coins and telephone cards. Cards can be purchased from post offices, tourist information kiosks and many shops. They are recommended for making international calls.

Time

The Bahamas and Jamaica keep US Eastern Standard Time (five hours behind Greenwich Mean Time). The rest of the Caribbean countries and Bermuda are one hour ahead of Eastern Standard Time (four hours behind GMT).

Tip your taxi driver!

Tipping

Although Caribbean hotel and restaurant bills generally include a service charge, personal tips are still expected by staff. Taxi drivers and restaurant staff anticipate a 10–15 per cent tip; a porter should receive around US$1 per piece of luggage.

Cruise passengers will also find a fairly aggressive tipping policy, as tips represent a significant portion of the cruise staff's income. Some top flight luxury cruise ships have abolished tipping, while others have a more relaxed optional gratuities policy, but most mainstream cruise lines provide tipping guidelines which are left in the cabin on the last night of the cruise, along with envelopes marked for the various recipients from the cabin steward to the *maître d'hôtel*.

Toilets

Public toilets are scarce in the islands, although they may be found near popular tourist sites. Hotels and restaurants will

DIRECTORY

usually allow non-patrons to use their restroom facilities, but it is polite to buy a drink if the toilet is in a pub or bar.

Tourist Offices

Island tourist offices are generally very helpful and willing to answer enquiries about accommodation, car rental, taxi fares, shopping and sports facilities, as well as providing maps and brochures containing local listings. In addition to the head offices listed below, there may be information kiosks at the airport, on the dockside and in other tourist areas.

Visitors who would like to receive information in advance of travel can contact the head offices direct. Many also have overseas branches in the US

Soaking up the rays in the beach paradise of Anguilla

and UK, and other countries that send a significant number of tourists to the region.

Anguilla: The Valley (tel: 809-497/2759).
Antigua: Thames Street, PO Box 363, St John's (tel: 268/462 0480).
Aruba: L G Smith Boulevard 172, PO Box 1019, Oranjestad (tel: 297-8/23777).
Bahamas: PO Box N3701, Nassau (tel: 242/322 7500).
Barbados: Harbour Road, PO Box 242, Bridgetown (tel: 246/427 2623).
Bermuda: Global House, PO Box HM 465, 43 Church Street, Hamilton HM BX (tel: 441/295 1480).

Bonaire: Kaya Simón Bolívar 12, Kralendijk (tel: 599-7/8322).
Cayman Islands: Harbour Centre, PO Box 67, North Church Street, George Town (tel: 345/949 0623).
Curaçao: Pietermaai 19, PO Box 3266, Willemstad (tel: 599-9/616000).
Dominica: Valley Road, PO Box 73, Roseau (tel: 809/448 2045).
Grenada: The Carenage, PO Box 293, St George's (tel: 809/440 2001).
Guadeloupe: 5 Square de la Banque, 97110 Pointe-à-Pitre (tel: 590/82 09 30).
Jamaica: 2 St Lucia Avenue, PO Box 360, Kingston (tel: 809/929 9200).
Martinique: rue Ernest Deproge, BP-520-97200, Fort-de-France (tel: 596/63 79 60).
Montserrat: Church Road, PO Box 7, Plymouth (tel: 869/491 2230).
Nevis: D R Walwyn Plaza, Main Street, Charlestown (tel: 869/469 1042).
Puerto Rico: La Casita, Calle Comercio, PO Box 4435, Old Town San Juan (tel: 787/722 1709).
Saba: The Post Office, Windwardside (tel: 599-4/62231).
St Barthélemy (St Barts): Mairie, place General de Gaulle, Gustavia (tel: 590/27 87 27).
St Kitts: Pelican Mall, PO Box 132, Basseterre (tel: 869/465 2620).
St Lucia: Pointe Seraphine, PO Box 221, Castries (tel: 758/452 4094).
Saint-Martin: Port de Marigot, 97150 Marigot (tel: 590/87 57 21).

St Vincent and the Grenadines: Department of Tourism Office, Bay Street, PO Box 834, Kingstown (tel: 809/457 1502).
Sint Eustatius (Statia): 3 Fort Street, Upper Town, Oranjestad (tel: 599-3/82433).
Sint Maarten: Walter Nisbeth Road 23, Philipsburg (tel: 599-5/22337).
Tobago: Tobago NIB Mall, Scarborough (tel: 868/639 2125).
Trinidad: 134 Frederick Street, Port of Spain (tel: 868/623 1932).
Virgin Islands (British): Social Security Building, Waterfront Street, Road Town, Tortola (tel: 809/494 3134).
Virgin Islands (US): PO Box 4538, Christiansted, St Croix (tel: 809/773 0495); PO Box 200, Cruz Bay, St John (tel: 809/776 6450); PO Box 6400, Charlotte Amalie, St Thomas (tel: 809/774 8784).

Visitors with Disabilities

The Caribbean islands are not very well prepared to handle the needs of visitors with disabilities. Tourist offices may be able to help with information about hotels with special facilities, but they are few and far between. Many hotels are built on hillsides with numerous steps and steep slopes to be negotiated. Few public buildings or restaurants have planned wheelchair access and kerbs are not modified.
Some cruise lines have taken a more positive attitude, and can offer a few cabins redesigned to achieve a wheelchair-friendly layout. However, enquiries for these facilities should be made well in advance.

LANGUAGE

To say that English is the official language of the former British colonies, Dutch is spoken in the Netherlands Antilles, and that they speak French on the French islands is only half the story. Visit ex-British Dominica or Dutch Sint Maarten and the local *patois* sounds like French until you listen in. In fact it is Creole, a French-African hybrid with borrowed words and phrases from half-a-dozen other languages, and widely spoken throughout the Windward and Leeward Islands. There are local variations from island to island, even from one side of an island to the other, and rapidly-spoken Creole is just as much of a mystery to a native French speaker as it is to other overseas visitors.

English speakers fare no better trying to decipher Jamaican or Antiguan *patois* with its English roots, and even language specialists are stumped by Papiamento, the bizarre dialect spoken in the Dutch Leewards (see page 58). However, English is the main language of the Caribbean tourism industry, though it is spoken little outside hotels in the French islands or in Spanish-speaking Puerto Rico where a phrase book would certainly come in handy. There are also *patois* phrase books on sale, and local people appreciate – or at the very least are largely entertained – if you try out a few words.

Relax, as the heat of the day gives way to a stunning sunset – a Caribbean speciality

INDEX

INDEX

INDEX/ACKNOWLEDGEMENTS

Acknowledgements

The Automobile Association wishes to thank the following photographers and libraries for their assistance in the preparation of this book:

JAMES HENDERSON 57, 58, 62, 65, 67
NATURE PHOTOGRAPHERS LTD 98 (P Sterry), 100a, 100c (K Carlson), 101a (P Sterry), 101b (Dr Michael Hill), 101c (S C Bisserot), 102 (P Sterry)
PICTURES COLOUR LIBRARY 61, 80/1, 82
SOPHIE CAMPBELL 86
SPECTRUM COLOUR LIBRARY 83, 85
ZEFA PICTURES LTD Cover

The remaining photographs are held in the Association's own library (AA PHOTO LIBRARY) and were taken by Peter Baker 4, 16, 19, 21, 25, 27, 29, 30, 33, 34, 35, 38/9, 41, 42/3, 45, 49, 50, 54, 69, 76, 77, 78, 95, 97, 107, 108/9, 109, 110/1, 119, 120, 121, 12; David Lyons 6, 7, 12, 22/3, 52, 70, 71, 72, 75, 93, 100b, 113, 124/5; Jon Wyand 8, 10, 11, 89, 90, 104, 105, 106, 114, 116 and Roy Victor 91, 103.

Contributors:
Copy editor: Audrey Horne   **Verifier:** James Ferguson
Designer: Dennis Buckley   **Indexer:** Marie Lorimer